My First Reading & Handwriting Workbook
ABCs
& Animal Friends

By Ms. Longneckgittimuspooharah

My First Reading & Handwriting Workbook

& Animal Friends

By Ms. Longneckgittimuspooharah

Copyright © 2021 by Ms. Longneckgittimuspooharah. All rights reserved. Copies are permitted for single classroom or home use by purchaser. Otherwise: This book or any portion thereof may not be reproduced or used in any manner whatsoever without the express written permission of the publisher except for brief quotations in a book or review.

Printed in the United States of America

First Printing: 2021

ISBN: 978-1-952674-15-0

Publisher: LeRoy Mac Publishing House

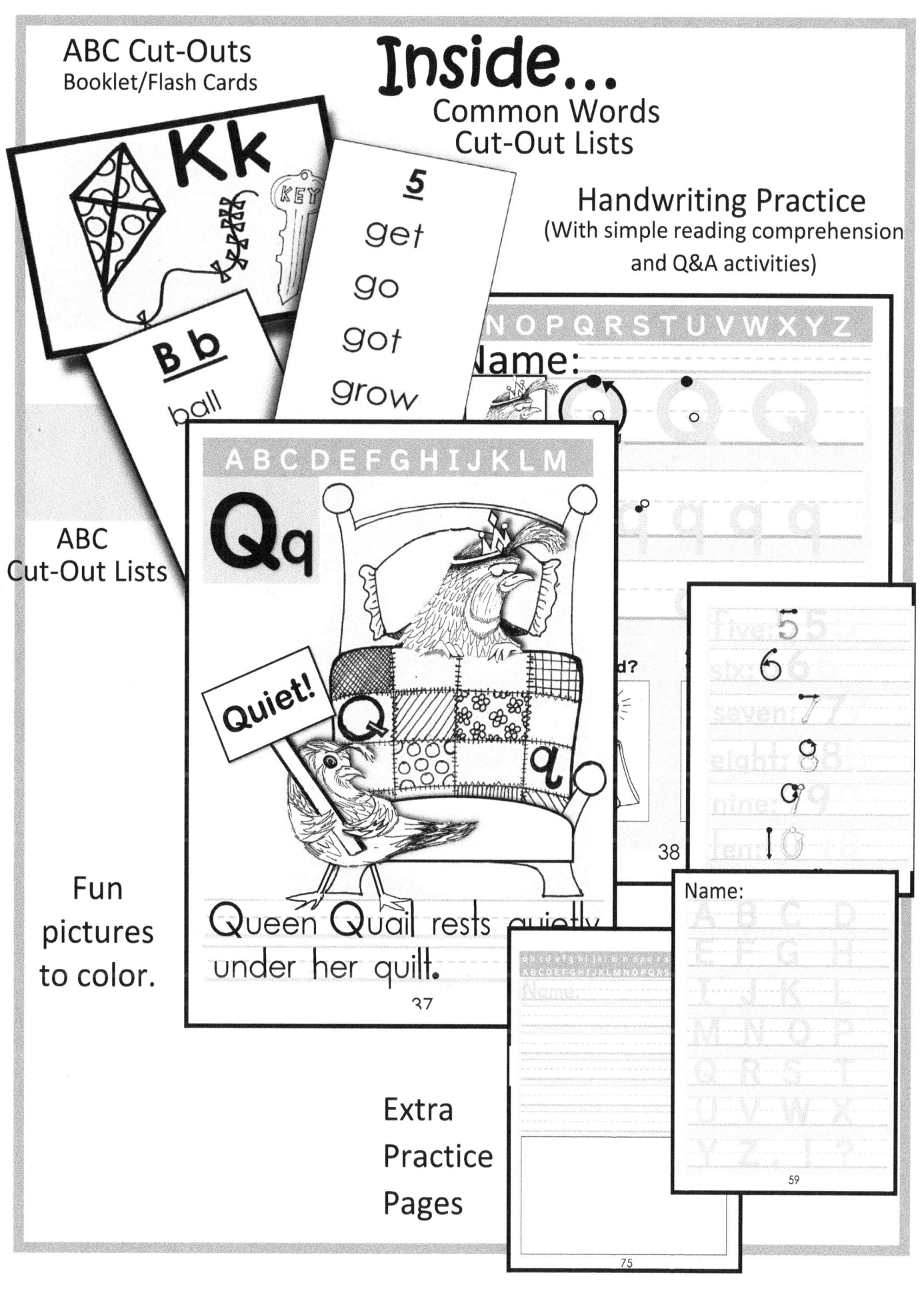

My First Reading & Handwriting Workbook

ABCs

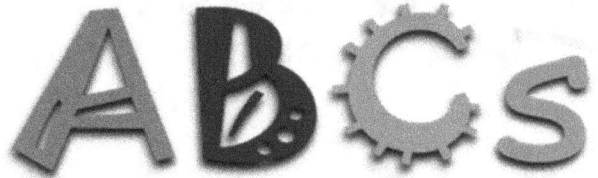

& Animal Friends

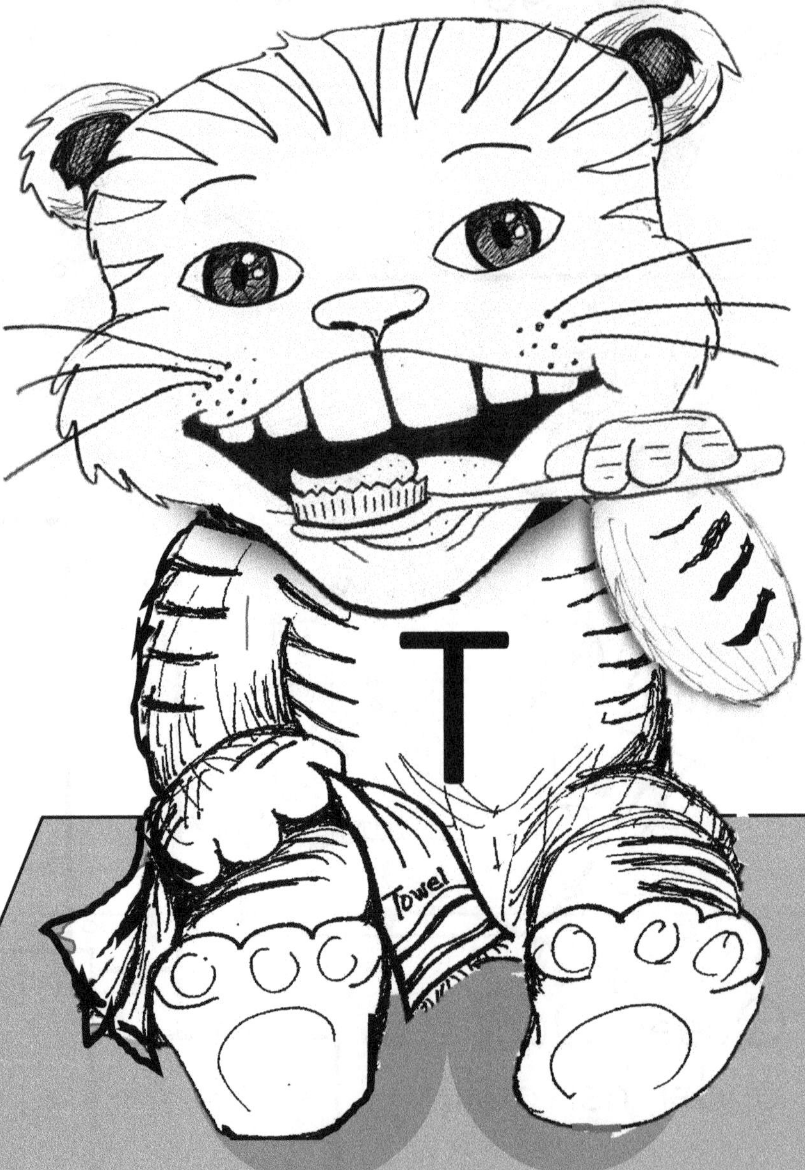

This book belongs to:

____

My First Reading & Handwriting Workbook

& Animal Friends

Table of Contents

Guide to the New, Simpler Handwriting Technique……..5-6

A-Z Reading and Handwriting Practice…………………….7-110

0-10 Tracing Practice……………………………………………..111-112

A-Z Tracing Practice………………………………………………113-114

Common Words Cut-Out Word Lists……………………..115-117

Alphabetized Cut-Out Lists……………………………………118-121

Alphabet Booklet/Flash Cards……………………………….121-124

Writing Ideas and Practice Pages………………………….125-133

Teaching Suggestions……………………………………………134

Picture Cut-Outs for ABC Pages…………………………….135-139

Guide to the New, Simpler Beginning Handwriting Technique

Typically, young learners follow various lines and numbers juxtaposed around letters and numerals as a first experience with handwriting. This new method uses an easier, color-based, less distracting guide to beginning handwriting. This may be especially beneficial to special needs learners. Three colors are used to help youngsters learn the correct path to write letters and numerals. The first line/curve to make is black. The second white. Third and fourth lines are grey. The lines/curves start at the dots, follow the direction of the arrows, and end at the triangles. The teacher/parent should make sure the youngster follows the correct path by modeling and explaining proper technique using the first letter on each practice page.

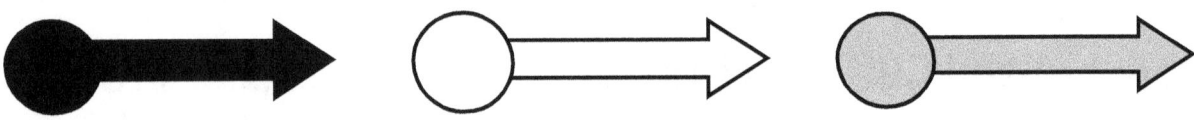

Simpler Beginning Handwriting Technique:

(1) pencil on the dot, follow the arrow

(2) black-white-grey

(3) say the letter and then the letter sound

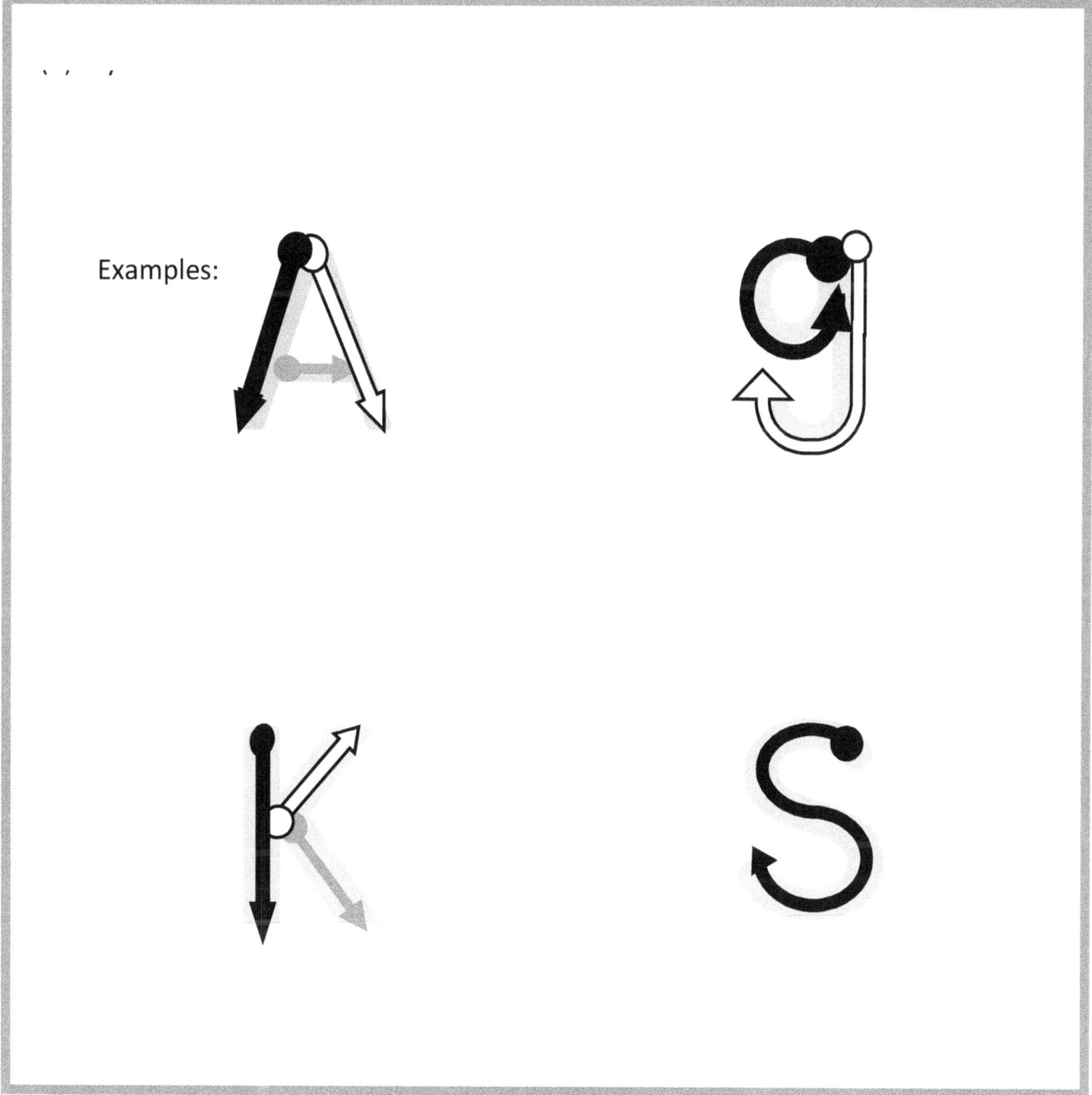

Examples:

My First Reading and Handwriting Workbook: ABCs & Animal Friends

Name: _____

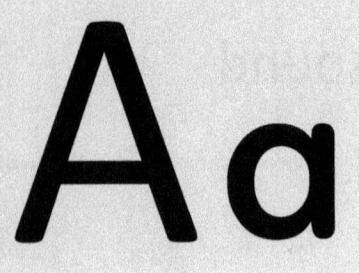

Use stick glue to glue one or more pictures of the letter and/or things that begin with the letter from packages, magazines, or online resources.

Name:

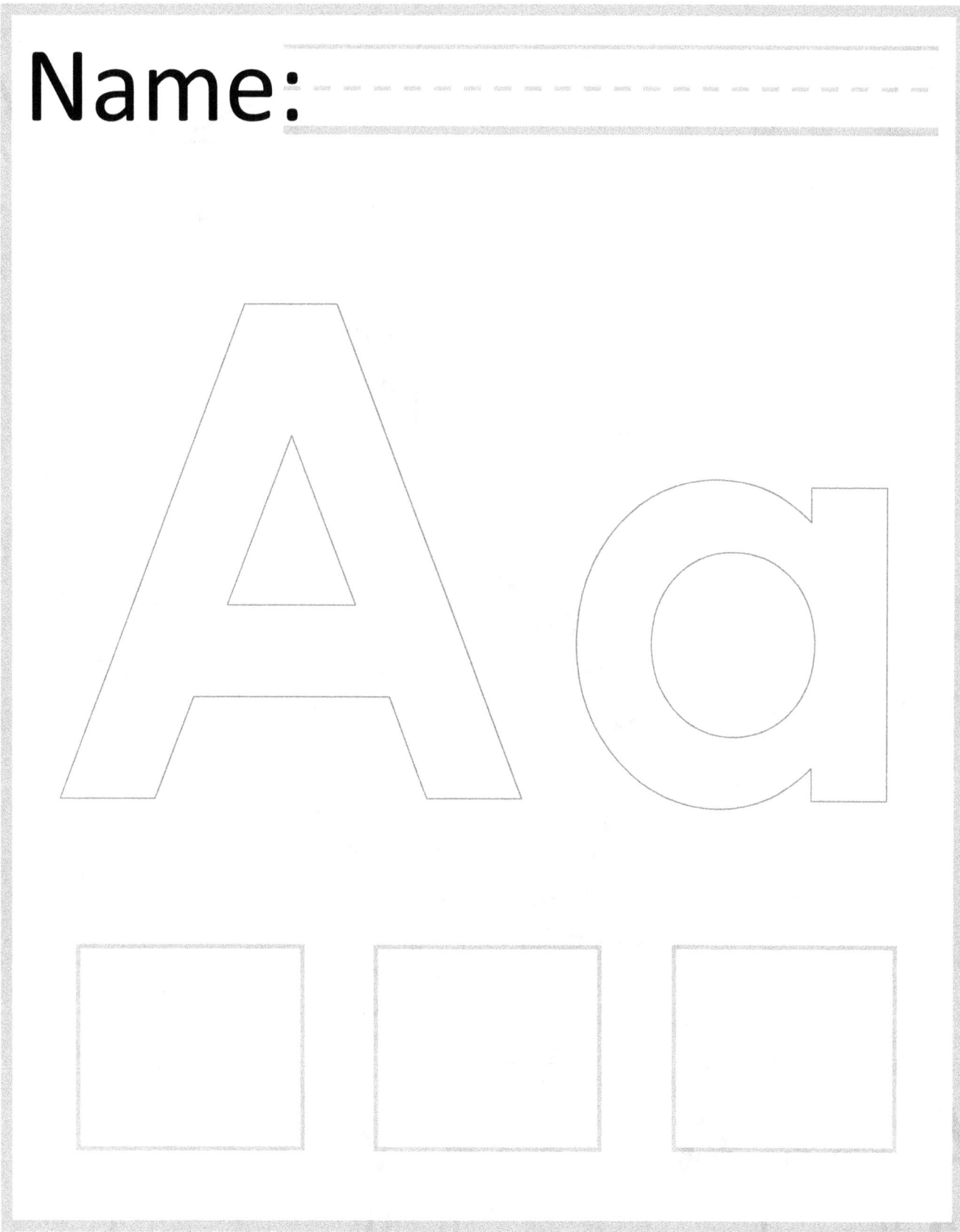

Color the letters. Then find the pictures at the back of the book that begin with the letter. Color the pictures and use stick glue to glue the pictures onto the squares.

A B C D E F G H I J K L M

Aa

Anna Ant and Alana Alligator ate all the apples.

N O P Q R S T U V W X Y Z

Name:

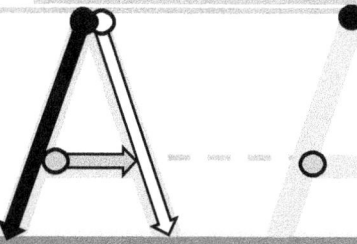

A a

How many apples did they eat in all? 6

10

Name:

B b

Use stick glue to glue one or more pictures of the letter and/or things that begin with the letter from packages, magazines, or online resources.

Name:

Color the letters. Then find the pictures at the back of the book that begin with the letter. Color the pictures and use stick glue to glue the pictures onto the squares.

A B C D E F G H I J K L M

B b

bananas

Buddy Bear has a blue ball and a brown boat.

N O P Q R S T U V W X Y Z

Name:

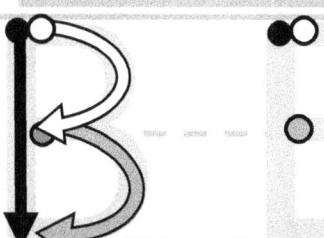
B B B B

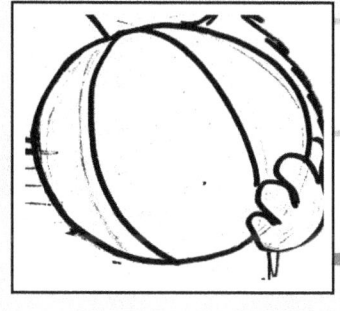
b b b b b

B b

What did Buddy
bring in a bucket
to the beach?

Circle one: bananas   berries

14

Name:

Cc

Use stick glue to glue one or more pictures of the letter and/or things that begin with the letter from packages, magazines, or online resources.

Name:

Cc

Color the letters. Then find the pictures at the back of the book that begin with the letter. Color the pictures and use stick glue to glue the pictures onto the squares.

A B C D E F G H I J K L M

Cc

Cally Cat likes to eat cookies, cake and carrots.

N O P Q R S T U V W X Y Z

Name:

C C C C

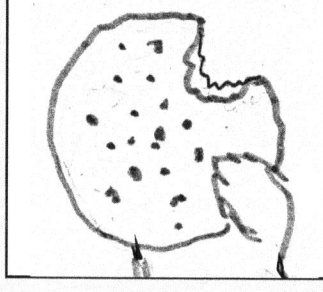

c c c c c

C c

Do you like cake or cookies better?

Circle one:

cake

cookies

Name:

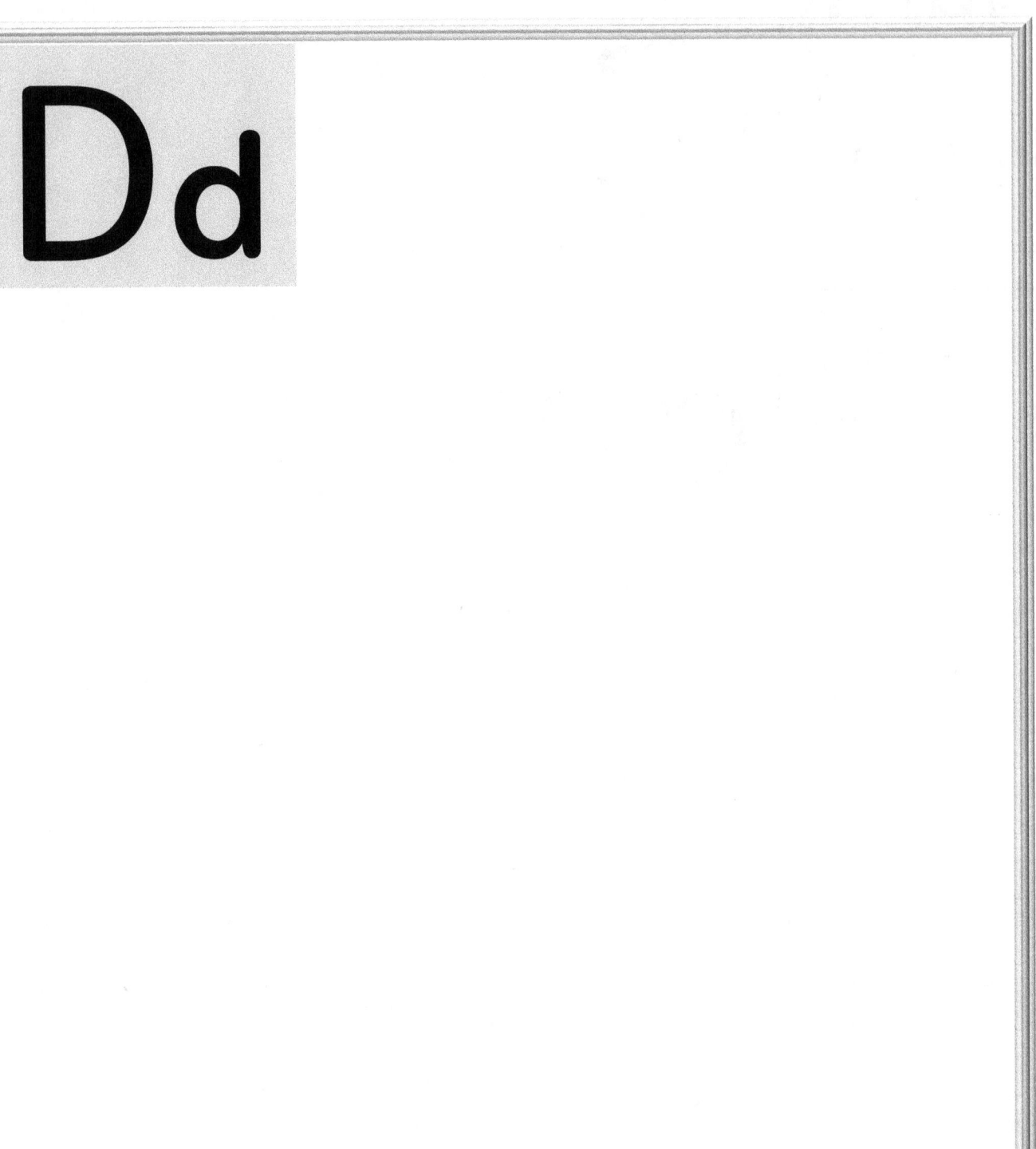

Use stick glue to glue one or more pictures of the letter and/or things that begin with the letter from packages, magazines, or online resources.

Name:

Color the letters. Then find the pictures at the back of the book that begin with the letter. Color the pictures and use stick glue to glue the pictures onto the squares.

A B C D E F G H I J K L M

Dd

Danny **D**og likes to draw and eat donuts.

N O P Q R S T U V W X Y Z

Name:

D D D D

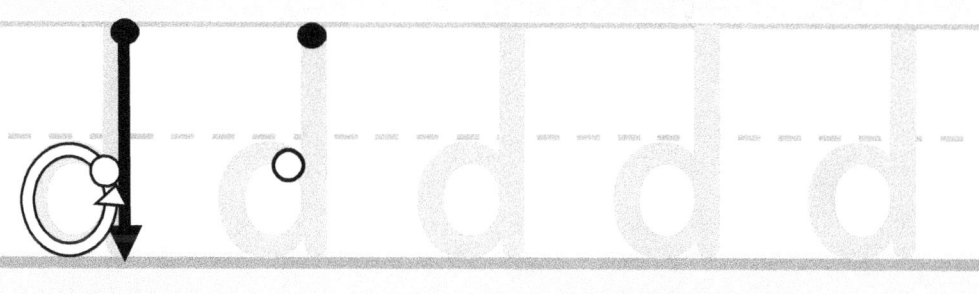

d d d d d

D d

What did Danny draw?

Circle yes or no under each picture.

a duck   a drum   a dinosaur   a door

 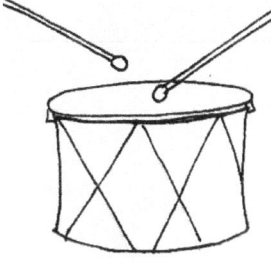  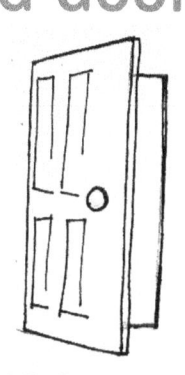

yes no   yes no   yes no   yes no

Name:

E e

Use stick glue to glue one or more pictures of the letter and/or things that begin with the letter from packages, magazines, or online resources.

Name: _____

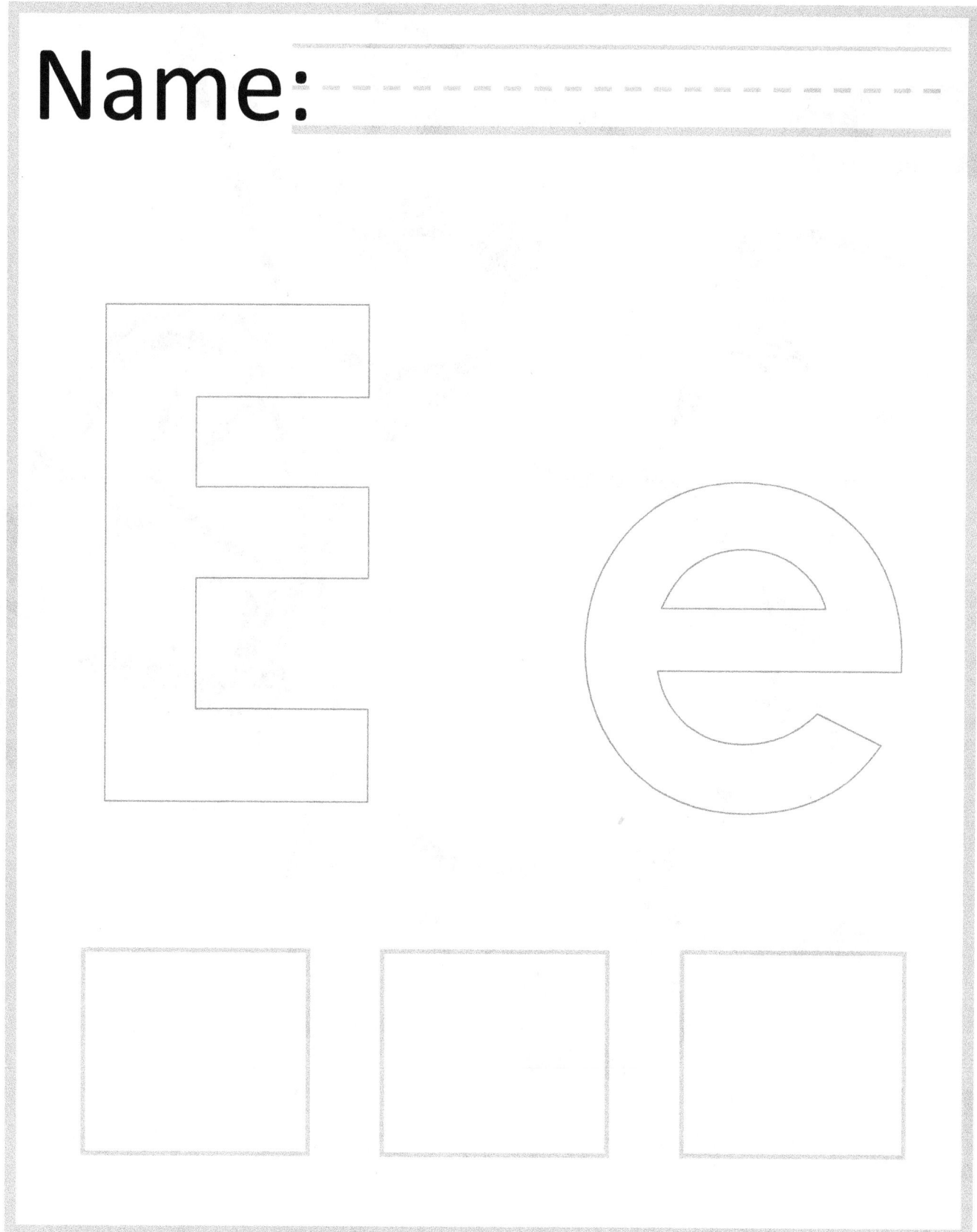

Color the letters. Then find the pictures at the back of the book that begin with the letter. Color the pictures and use stick glue to glue the pictures onto the squares.

A B C D E F G H I J K L M

Ee

Elle Elephant eats three big eggs everyday.

N O P Q R S T U V W X Y Z

Name:

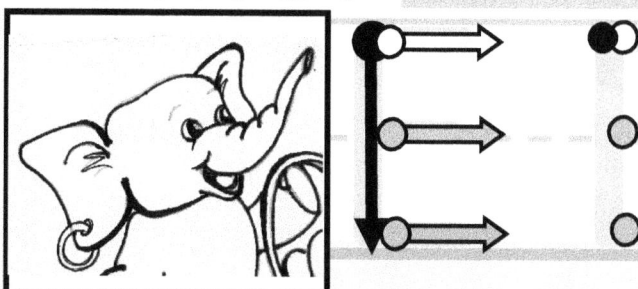

E E E E

   e e e e

E

e

Do you eat eggs?

Circle: Yes or No

Name:

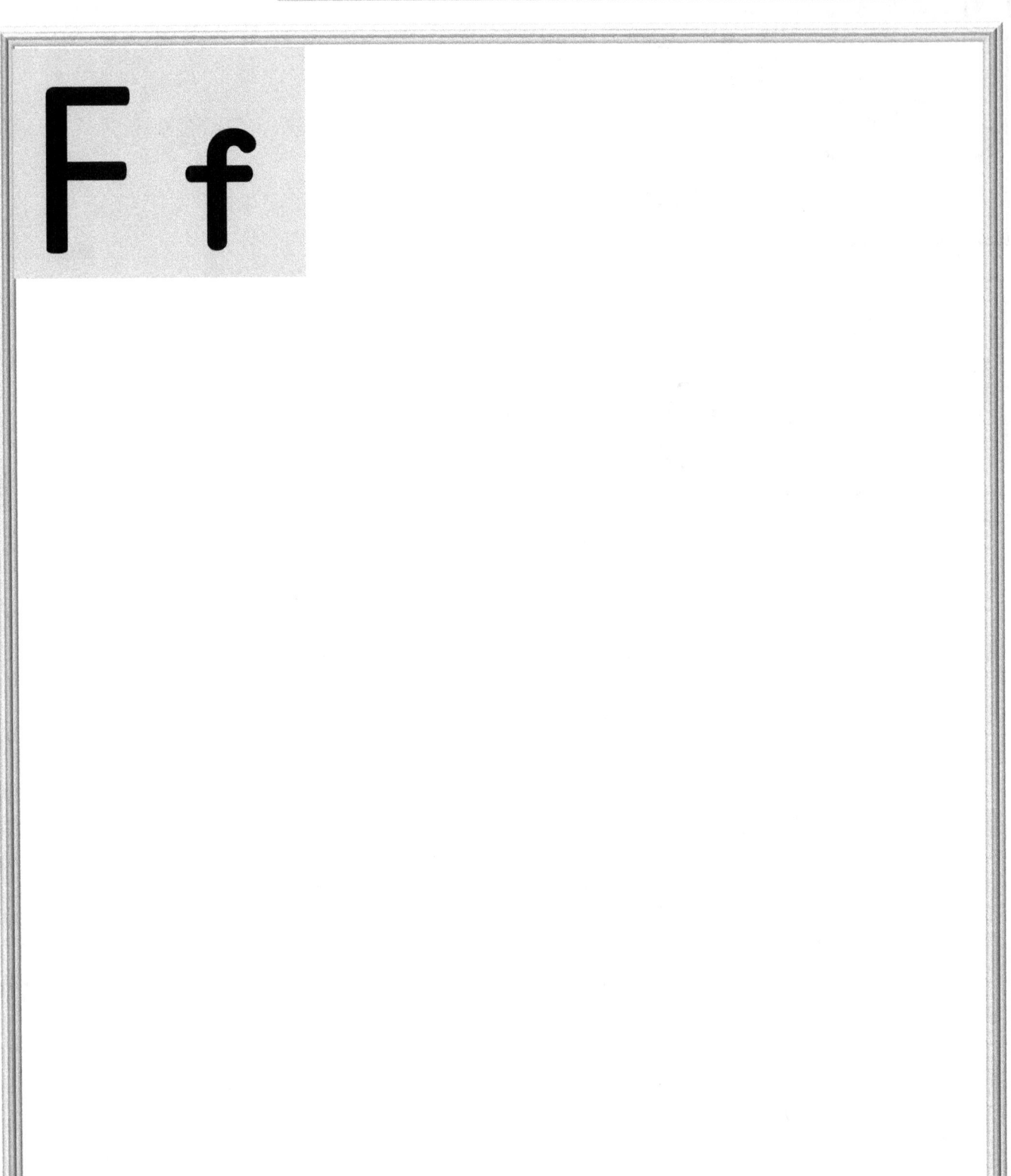

Use stick glue to glue one or more pictures of the letter and/or things that begin with the letter from packages, magazines, or online resources.

Name:

Color the letters. Then find the pictures at the back of the book that begin with the letter. Color the pictures and use stick glue to glue the pictures onto the squares.

A B C D E F G H I J K L M

F f

Frances Fish has fun with a flower friend.

N O P Q R S T U V W X Y Z

Name:

 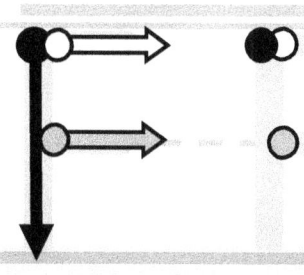

F F F F F F F F

 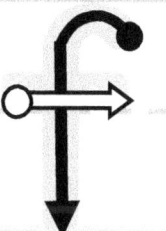

f f f f f f f f

Assist the student, if necessary, to complete the drawings below. Or draw for student to trace.

Draw a funny face.   **Draw funny feet.**

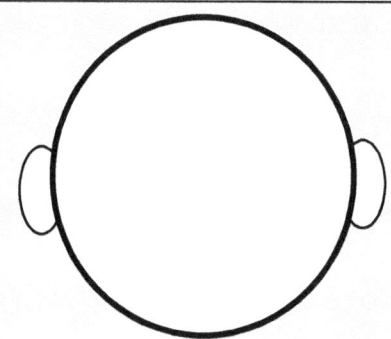

30

Name:

Gg

Use stick glue to glue one or more pictures of the letter and/or things that begin with the letter from packages, magazines, or online resources.

Name:

Color the letters. Then find the pictures at the back of the book that begin with the letter. Color the pictures and use stick glue to glue the pictures onto the squares.

A B C D E F G H I J K L M
Gg

Gary Goat gobbles green grapes in the green grass.

N O P Q R S T U V W X Y Z

Name:

 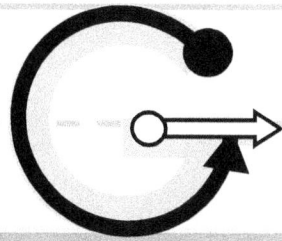 G 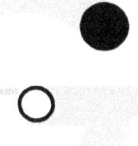 G

  g  g g g

G g

Where can you go to
get grapes ?

garage

grocery

gym

garden

Name:

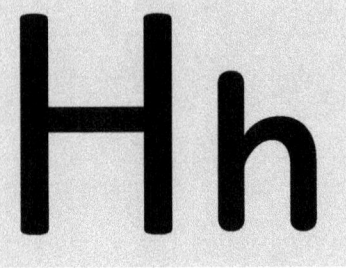

Use stick glue to glue one or more pictures of the letter and/or things that begin with the letter from packages, magazines, or online resources.

Name:

Color the letters. Then find the pictures at the back of the book that begin with the letter. Color the pictures and use stick glue to glue the pictures onto the squares.

A B C D E F G H I J K L M

Hh

Hal Horse is happy. He has his new hats on his head.

N O P Q R S T U V W X Y Z

Name:

H H H H H

h h h h h

H h

How many hats does Hal have on his head? 4

Name:

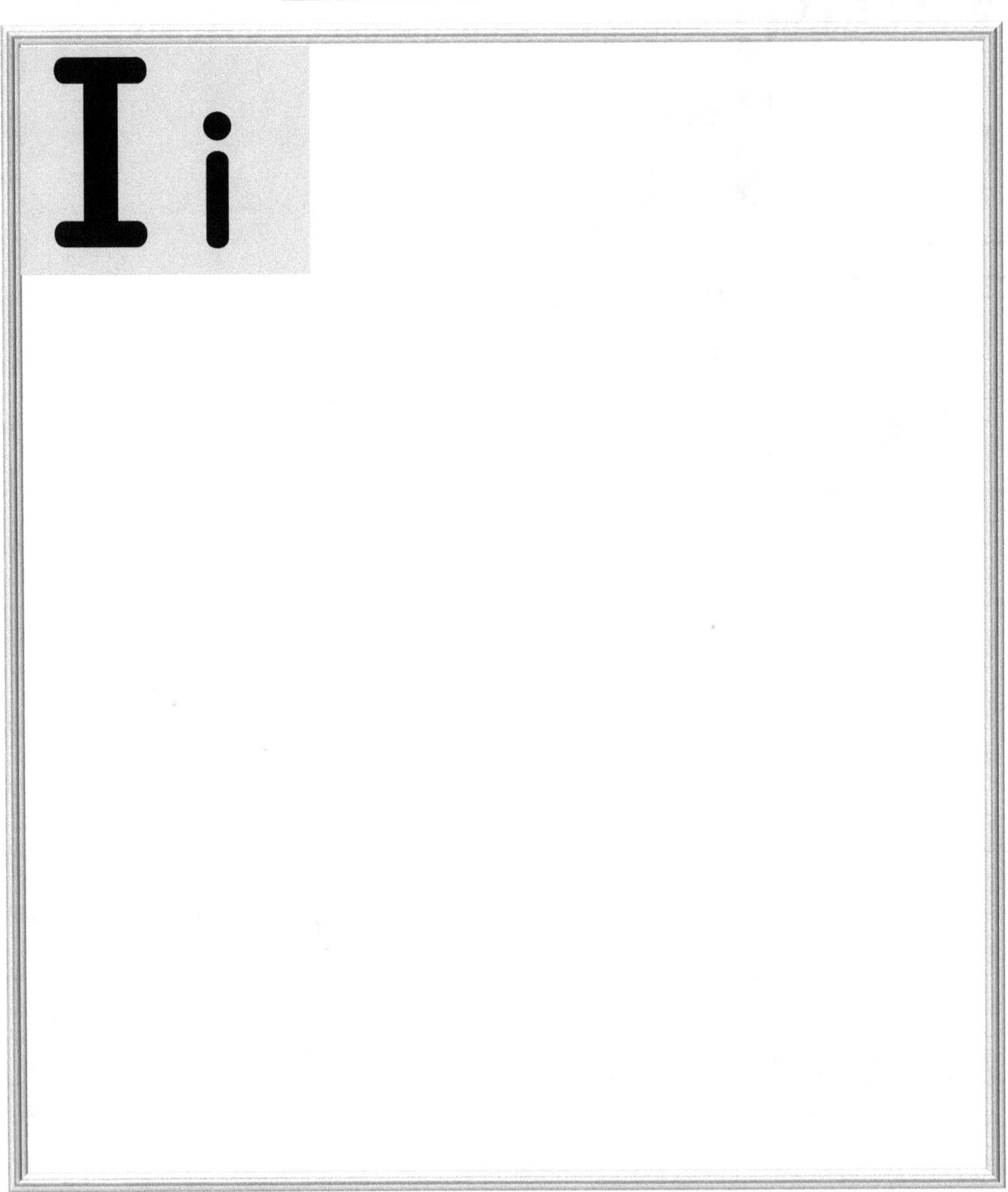

Use stick glue to glue one or more pictures of the letter and/or things that begin with the letter from packages, magazines, or online resources.

Name:

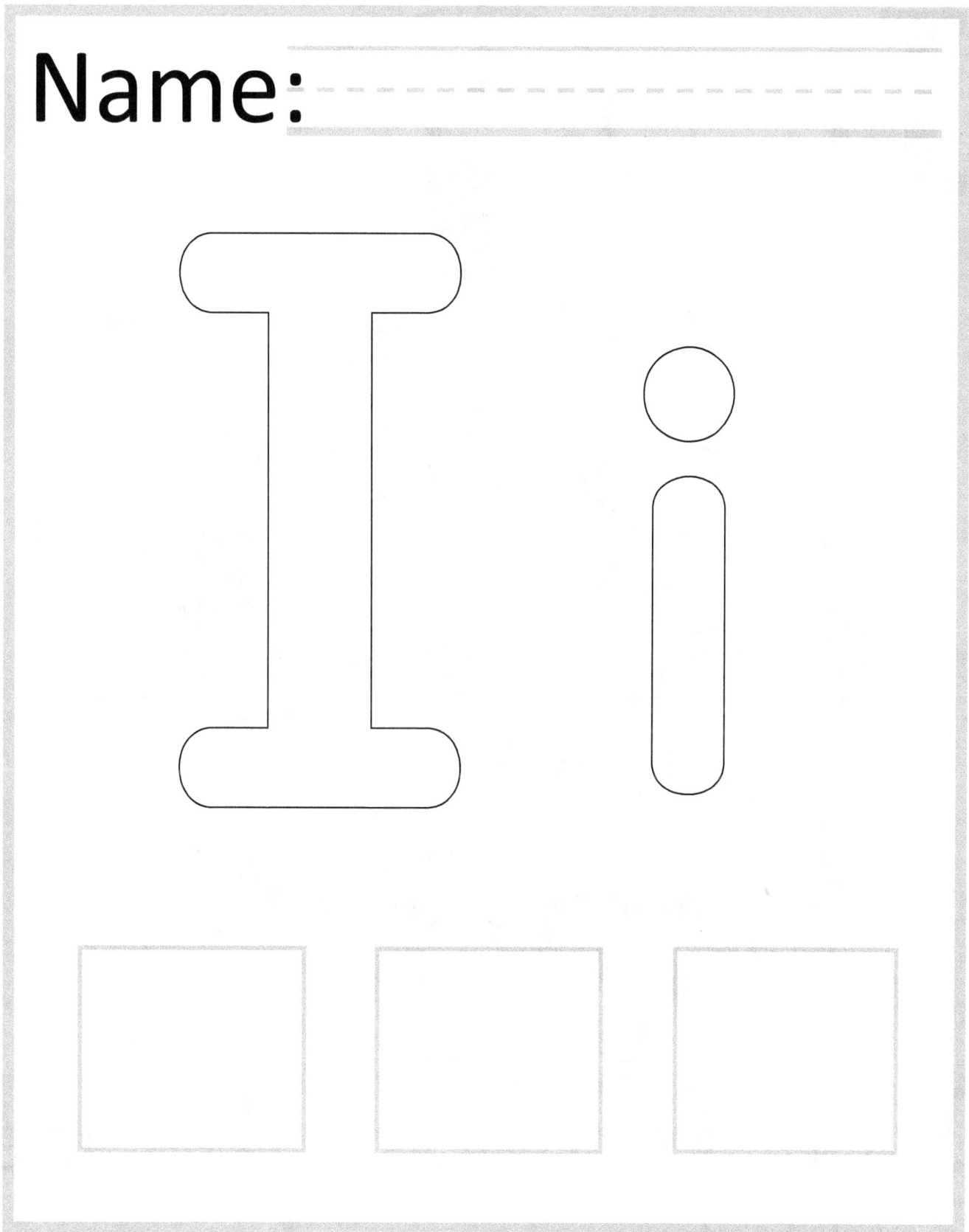

Color the letters. Then find the pictures at the back of the book that begin with the letter. Color the pictures and use stick glue to glue the pictures onto the squares.

A B C D E F G H I J K L M
Ii

Ivan Inchworm likes ice on his ice cream!

N O P Q R S T U V W X Y Z

Name:

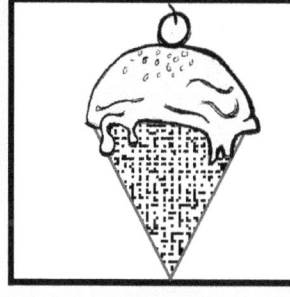
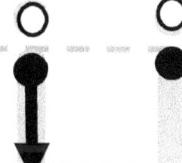

I i

Is ice cream better in a cup or in a cone?

Circle the one
you think is better: cup   cone

42

Name: ------------------

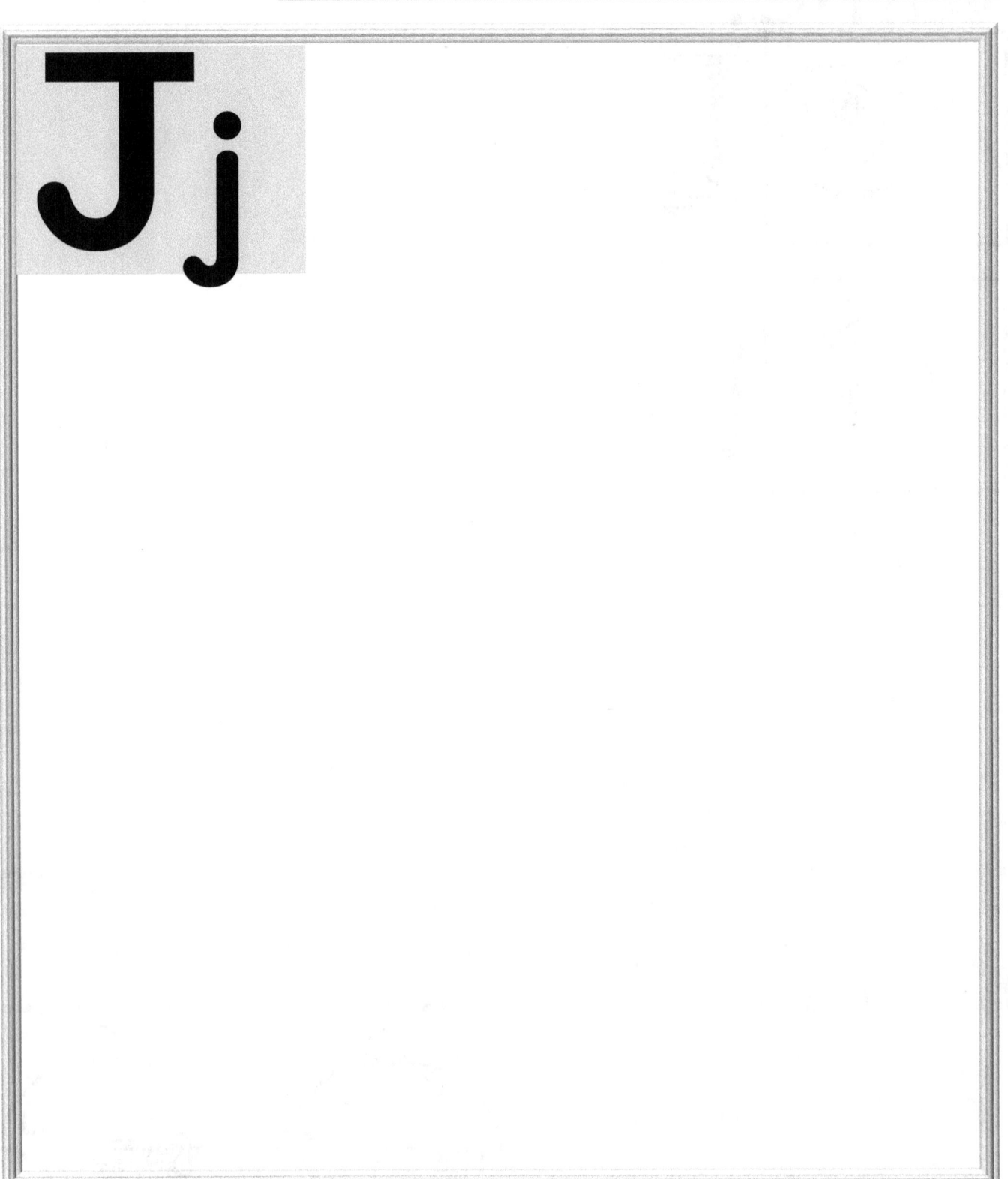

Use stick glue to glue one or more pictures of the letter and/or things that begin with the letter from packages, magazines, or online resources.

Name:

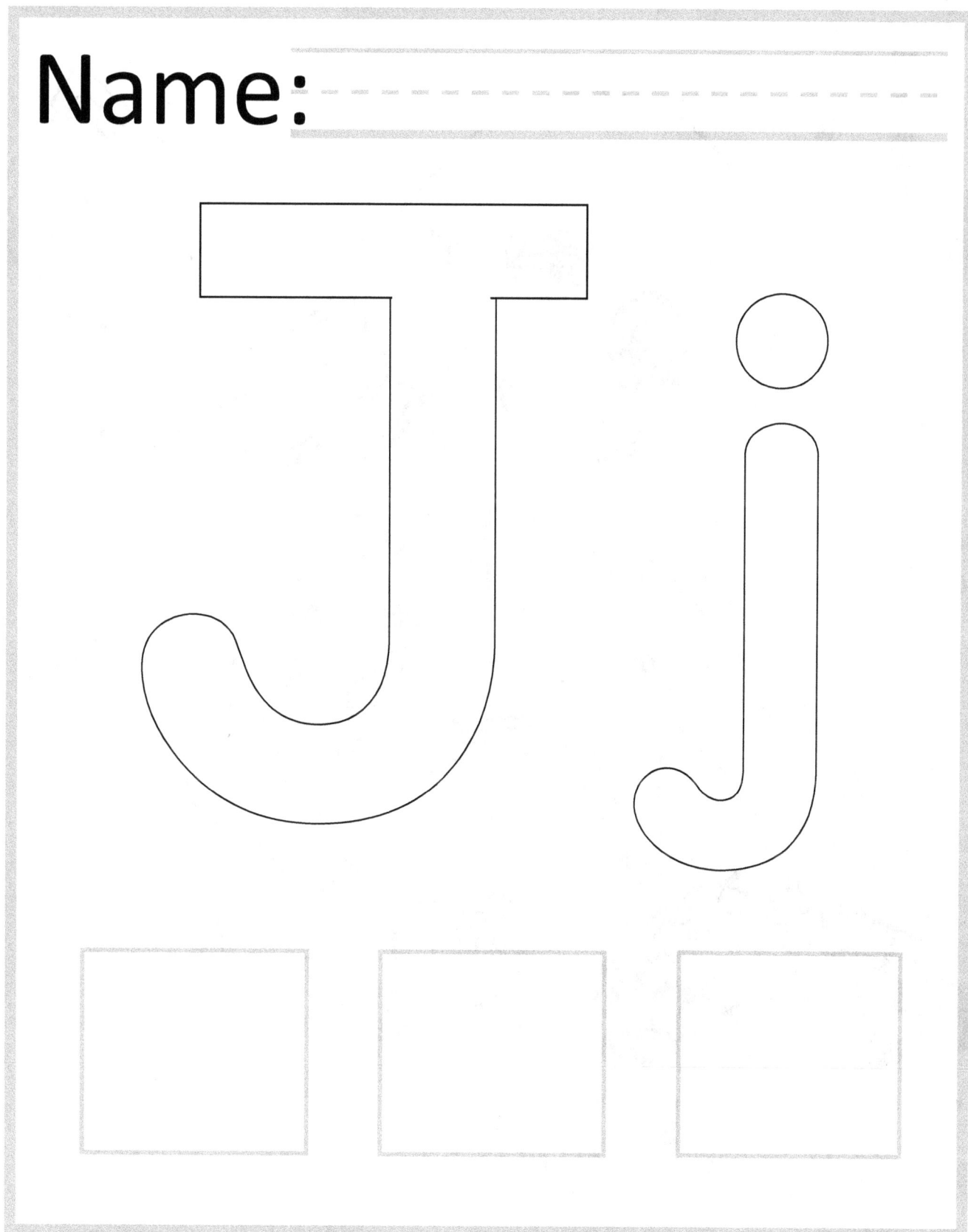

Color the letters. Then find the pictures at the back of the book that begin with the letter. Color the pictures and use stick glue to glue the pictures onto the squares.

A B C D E F G H I J K L M
Jj

Jenny Jellyfish has juice with jam and jellybeans.

NOPQRSTUVWXYZ

Name:

J J J J J

j j j j j

Jenny gave Jaguar a jar of j

46

Name: ----------------

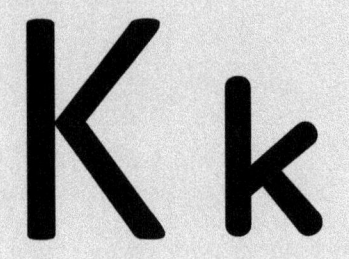

Use stick glue to glue one or more pictures of the letter and/or things that begin with the letter from packages, magazines, or online resources.

47

Name:

Color the letters. Then find the pictures at the back of the book that begin with the letter. Color the pictures and use stick glue to glue the pictures onto the squares.

A B C D E F G H I J K L M

Kk

Kanga Kangaroo keeps keys and tiny kites.

N O P Q R S T U V W X Y Z

Name:

 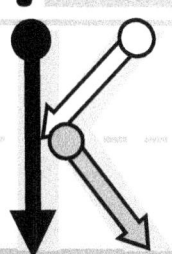 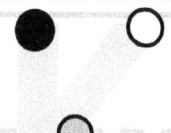 K K K

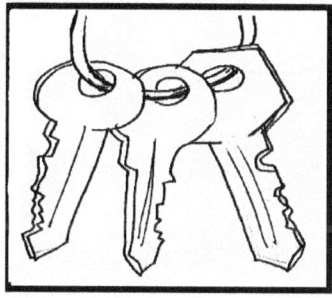  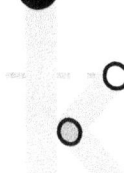 k k k

K k

How many keys does Kanga have?

 4 + 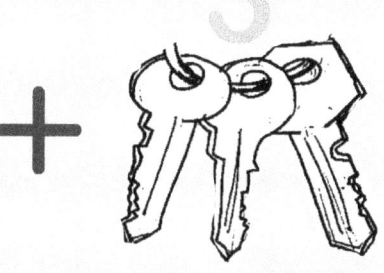 3 =  7

Name:

Ll

Use stick glue to glue one or more pictures of the letter and/or things that begin with the letter from packages, magazines, or online resources.

Name:

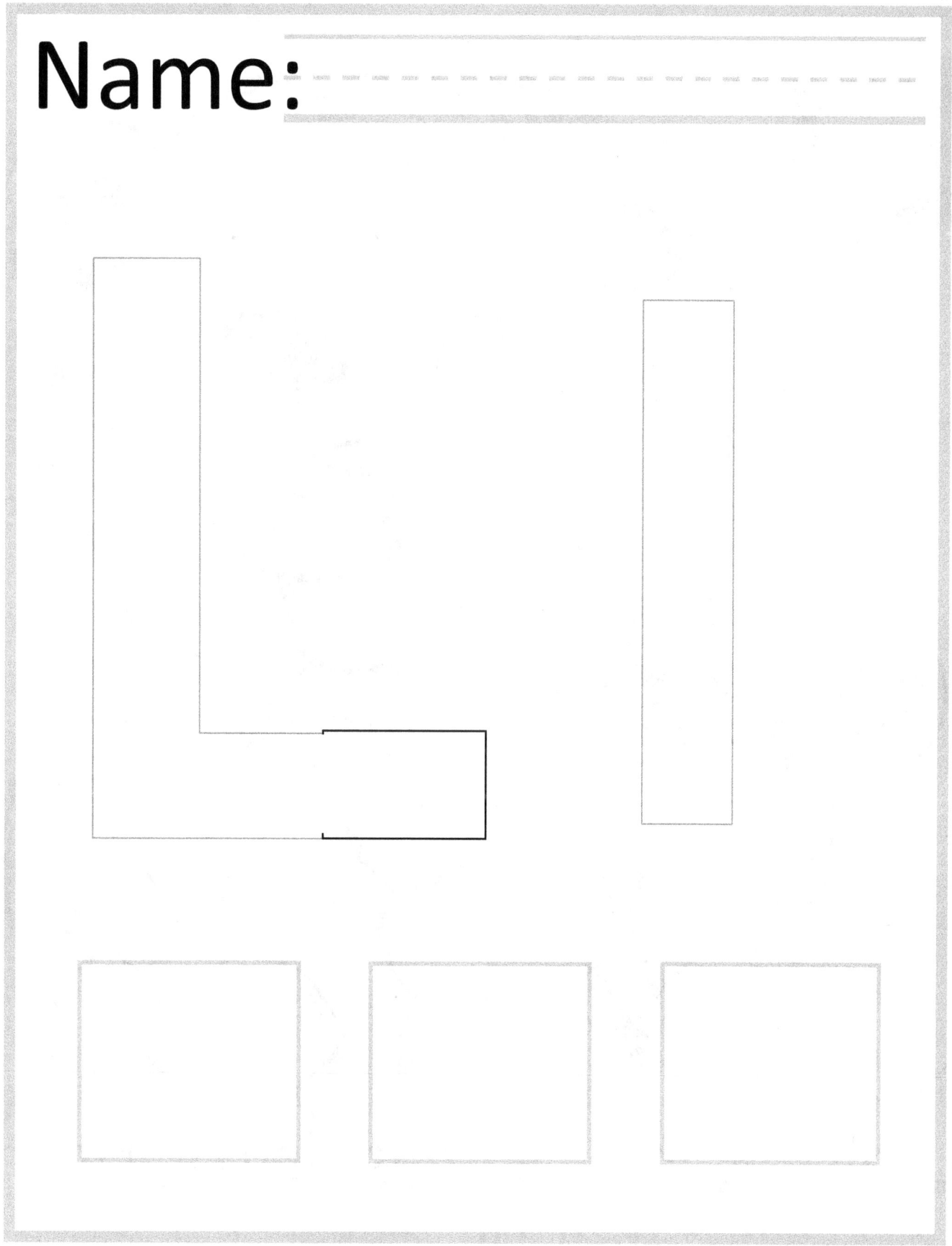

Color the letters. Then find the pictures at the back of the book that begin with the letter. Color the pictures and use stick glue to glue the pictures onto the squares.

A B C D E F G H I J K L M

Ll

Lala Lion loves lemons, limes, and lollipops.

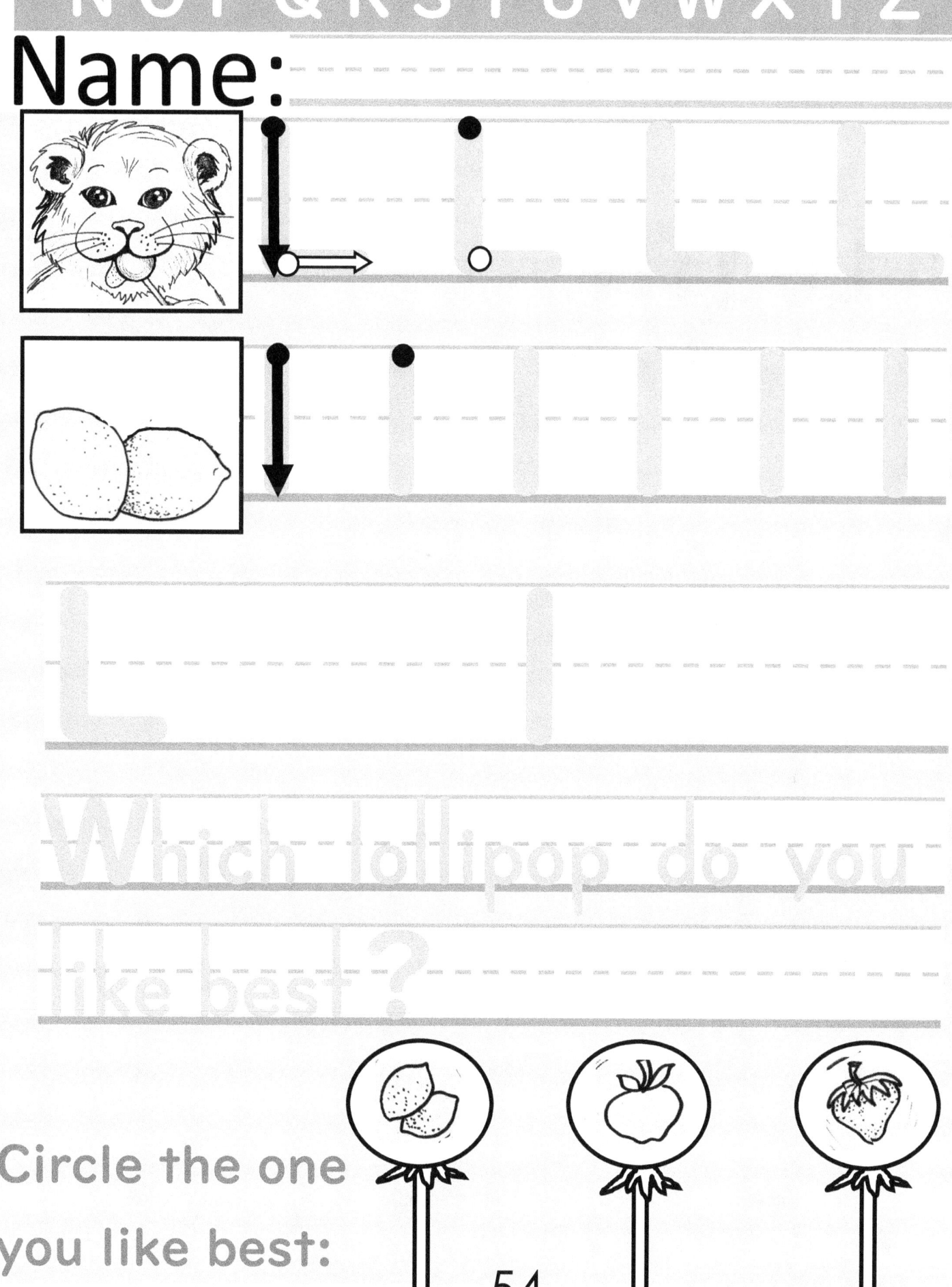

Name:

Use stick glue to glue one or more pictures of the letter and/or things that begin with the letter from packages, magazines, or online resources.

Name:

Mm

Color the letters. Then find the pictures at the back of the book that begin with the letter. Color the pictures and use stick glue to glue the pictures onto the squares.

ABCDEFGHIJKLM

Mm

Molly Monkey and Manny Mouse make music. Then they munch on muffins.

N O P Q R S T U V W X Y Z

Name:

 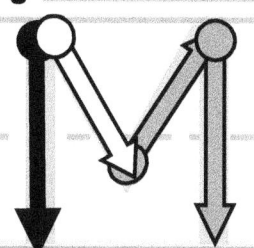 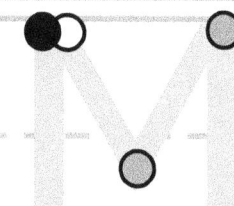 M M

 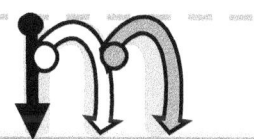 m m m

M m

Who had more food?

Molly had more food.

Trace the lines to each friend's food.

less

more

Name:

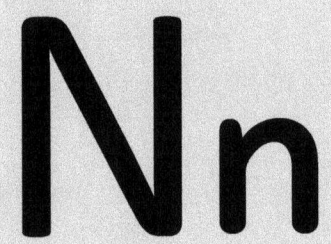

Use stick glue to glue one or more pictures of the letter and/or things that begin with the letter from packages, magazines, or online resources.

Name: _____

Color the letters. Then find the pictures at the back of the book that begin with the letter. Color the pictures and use stick glue to glue the pictures onto the squares.

A B C D E F G H I J K L M

Nn

Nilly Nighthawk has a nice necklace on her neck.

N O P Q R S T U V W X Y Z

Name:

 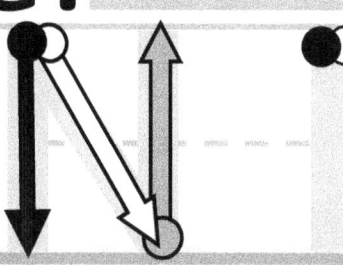 

N N N N

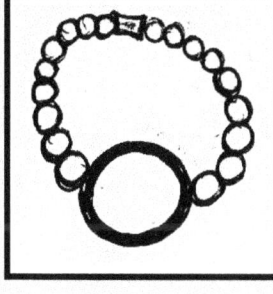  n n n n n

N n

Draw a nose and a neck.

Nick needs a **nose.**

Nick needs a **neck.**

62

Name:

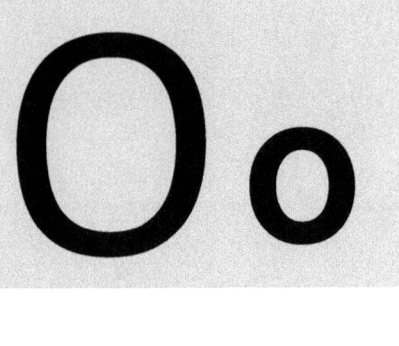

Use stick glue to glue one or more pictures of the letter and/or things that begin with the letter from packages, magazines, or online resources.

Name:

Color the letters. Then find the pictures at the back of the book that begin with the letter. Color the pictures and use stick glue to glue the pictures onto the squares.

A B C D E F G H I J K L M

Oo

Oscar Octopus got his oranges out of the ocean!

N O P Q R S T U V W X Y Z

Name:

O O O

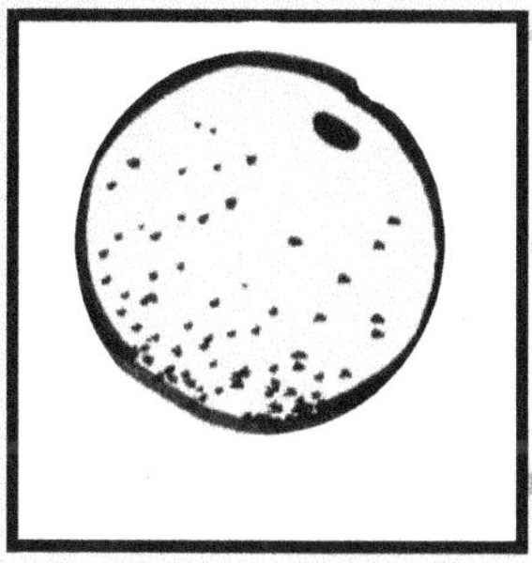

o o o o o o

O o

How do oranges grow?

An octopus grows oranges in the ocean?	A farmer grows oranges on trees?
Yes No	Yes No

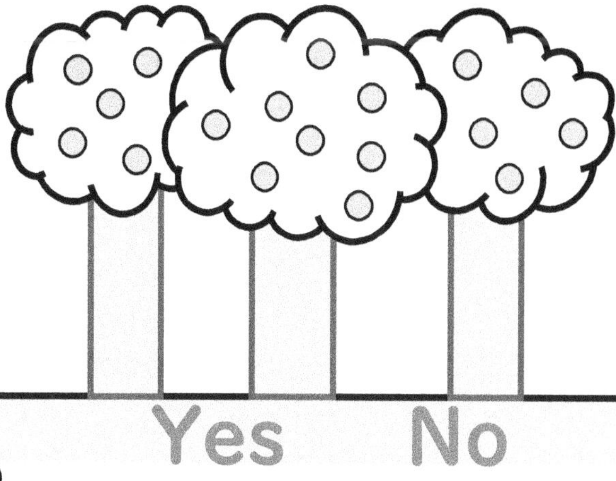

Name:

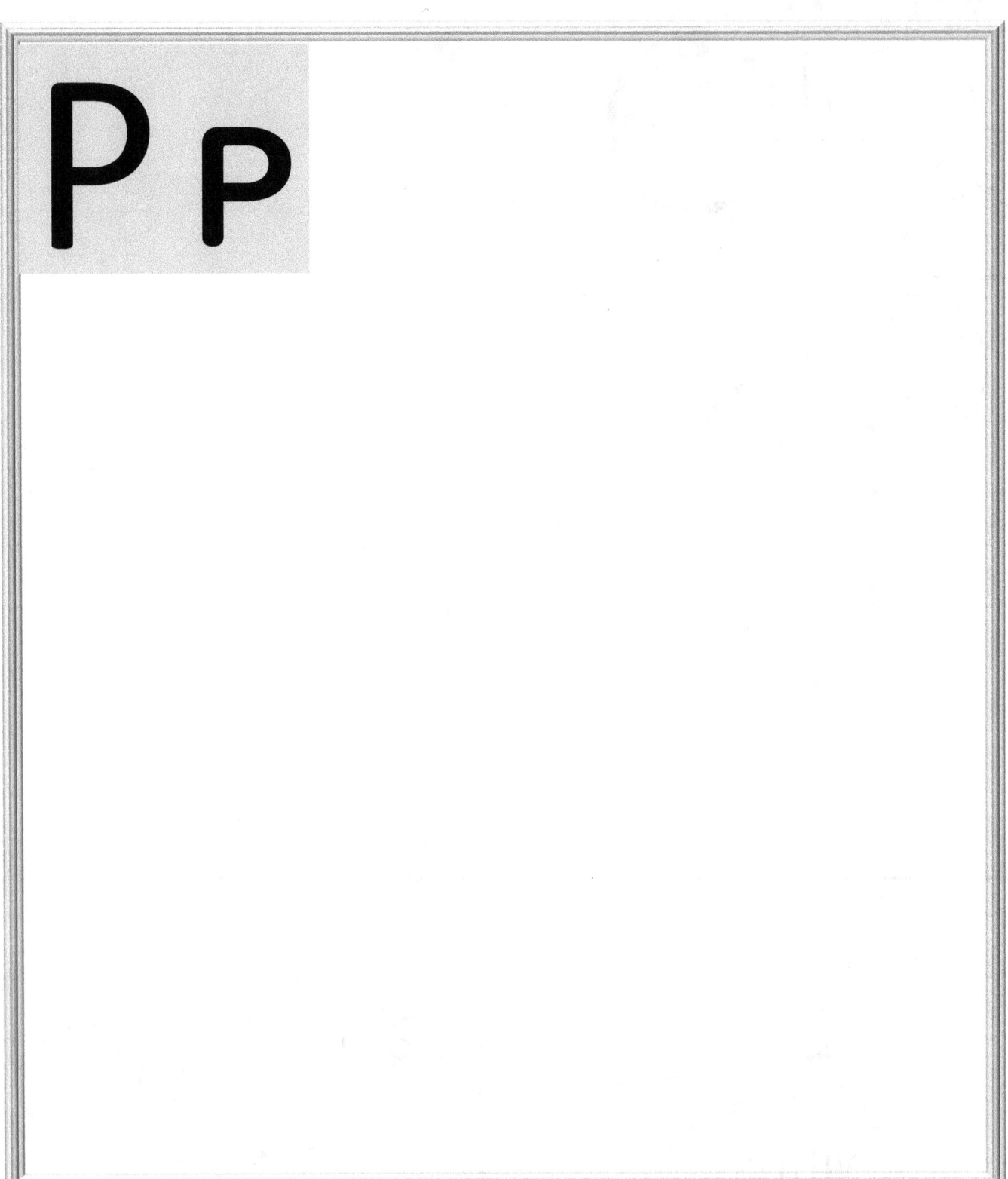

Use stick glue to glue one or more pictures of the letter and/or things that begin with the letter from packages, magazines, or online resources.

Name: _____

Color the letters. Then find the pictures at the back of the book that begin with the letter. Color the pictures and use stick glue to glue the pictures onto the squares.

ABCDEFGHIJKLM

P p

Pam Pig loves popcorn and pink and purple crayons.

N O P Q R S T U V W X Y Z

Name:

P P P P

p p p p

P p

Color this   Color this

paint pink.   paint purple.

70

Name:

Use stick glue to glue one or more pictures of the letter and/or things that begin with the letter from packages, magazines, or online resources.

Name:

Color the letters. Then find the pictures at the back of the book that begin with the letter. Color the pictures and use stick glue to glue the pictures onto the squares.

A B C D E F G H I J K L M

Qq

Queen Quail rests quietly under her quilt.

N O P Q R S T U V W X Y Z

Name:

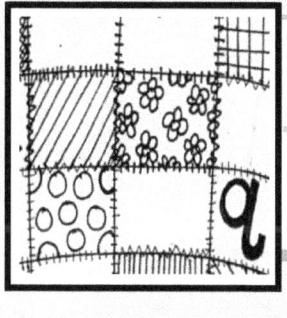

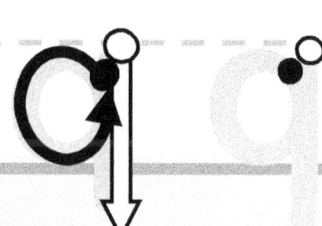
Q Q Q

q q q q

Q q

Answer the **questions**.

Are you **quiet** on the playground?

Are you **quiet** when you sleep?

Yes   No

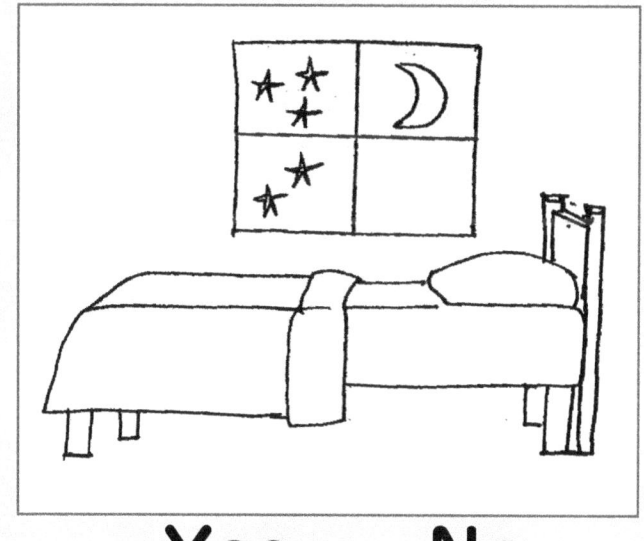

Yes   No

74

Name:

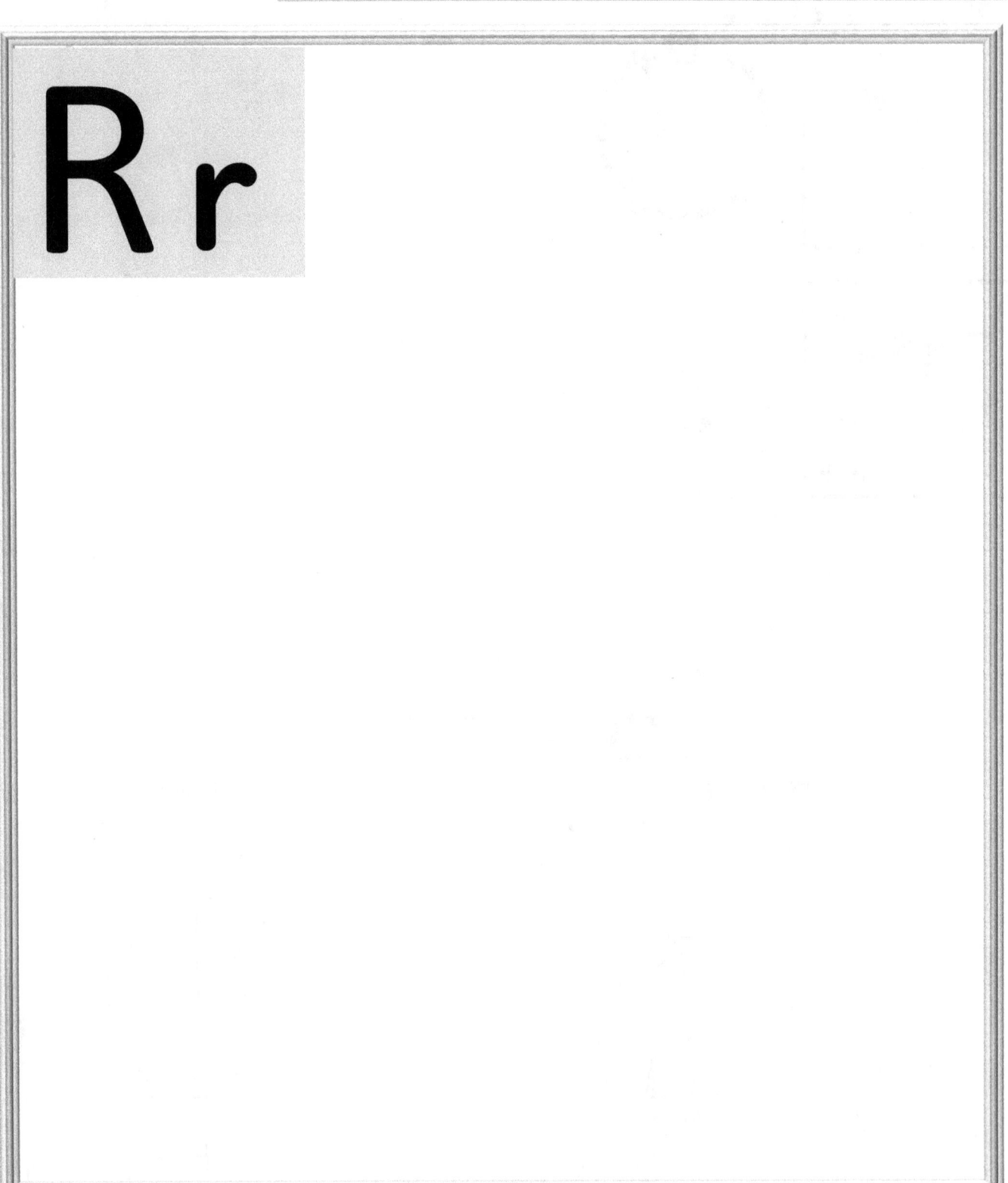

Use stick glue to glue one or more pictures of the letter and/or things that begin with the letter from packages, magazines, or online resources.

Name: _____

Color the letters. Then find the pictures at the back of the book that begin with the letter. Color the pictures and use stick glue to glue the pictures onto the squares.

ABCDEFGHIJKLM

Rr

Randy Rabbit ran a race in the rain. He won a red ribbon and three red roses.

N O P Q R S T U V W X Y Z

Name:

R R R R R

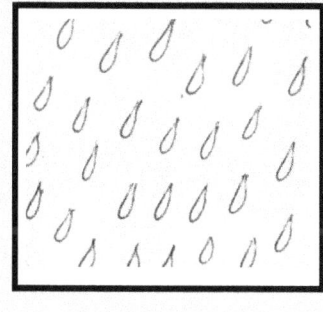 

r r r r r r

R r

Question: What did Randy get for his reward?

Answer: Randy won a

and 3.

Name:

S s

Use stick glue to glue one or more pictures of the letter and/or things that begin with the letter from packages, magazines, or online resources.

Name:

Color the letters. Then find the pictures at the back of the book that begin with the letter. Color the pictures and use stick glue to glue the pictures onto the squares.

A B C D E F G H I J K L M

S s

Sammy **S**nake snacks on a sandwich in a sock!

N O P Q R S T U V W X Y Z

Name:

S s s s s

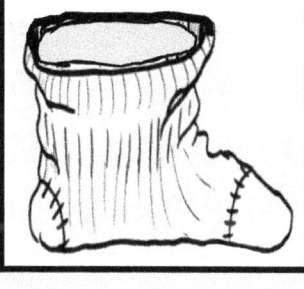

s s s s s

"This snack is so good!" Sammy said. "What do you like for a snack?"

82

Name: ----------------

Use stick glue to glue one or more pictures of the letter and/or things that begin with the letter from packages, magazines, or online resources.

Name: _____

Color the letters. Then find the pictures at the back of the book that begin with the letter. Color the pictures and use stick glue to glue the pictures onto the squares.

A B C D E F G H I J K L M

T t

Tammy Turtle is teaching Tommy Tiger how to take care of his teeth. "Brush every tooth," said Tammy.

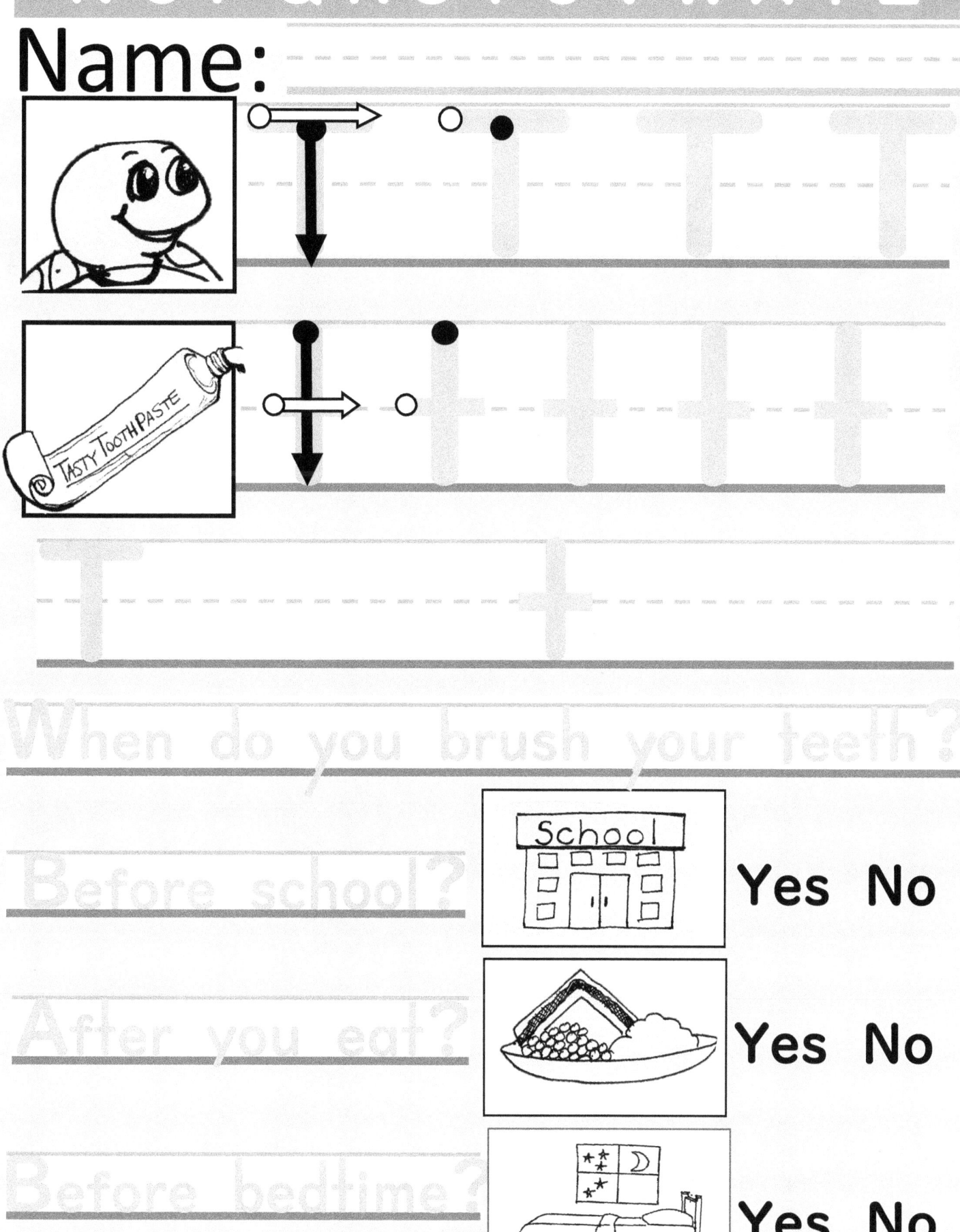

Name:

Use stick glue to glue one or more pictures of the letter and/or things that begin with the letter from packages, magazines, or online resources.

Name:

U u

Color the letters. Then find the pictures at the back of the book that begin with the letter. Color the pictures and use stick glue to glue the pictures onto the squares.

A B C D E F G H I J K L M

Uu

Unis **U**nicorn likes to jump under her umbrella.

N O P Q R S T U V W X Y Z

Name:

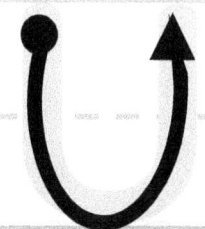
U U U U

u u u u

U u

"Can you come over?" Unis asked Hal. "My Uncle Usie will let us use a big umbrella!"

"Your uncle has a cool umbrella!" Hal said.

"Have you ever been under a big umbrella?"
   Yes   or   No

Name:

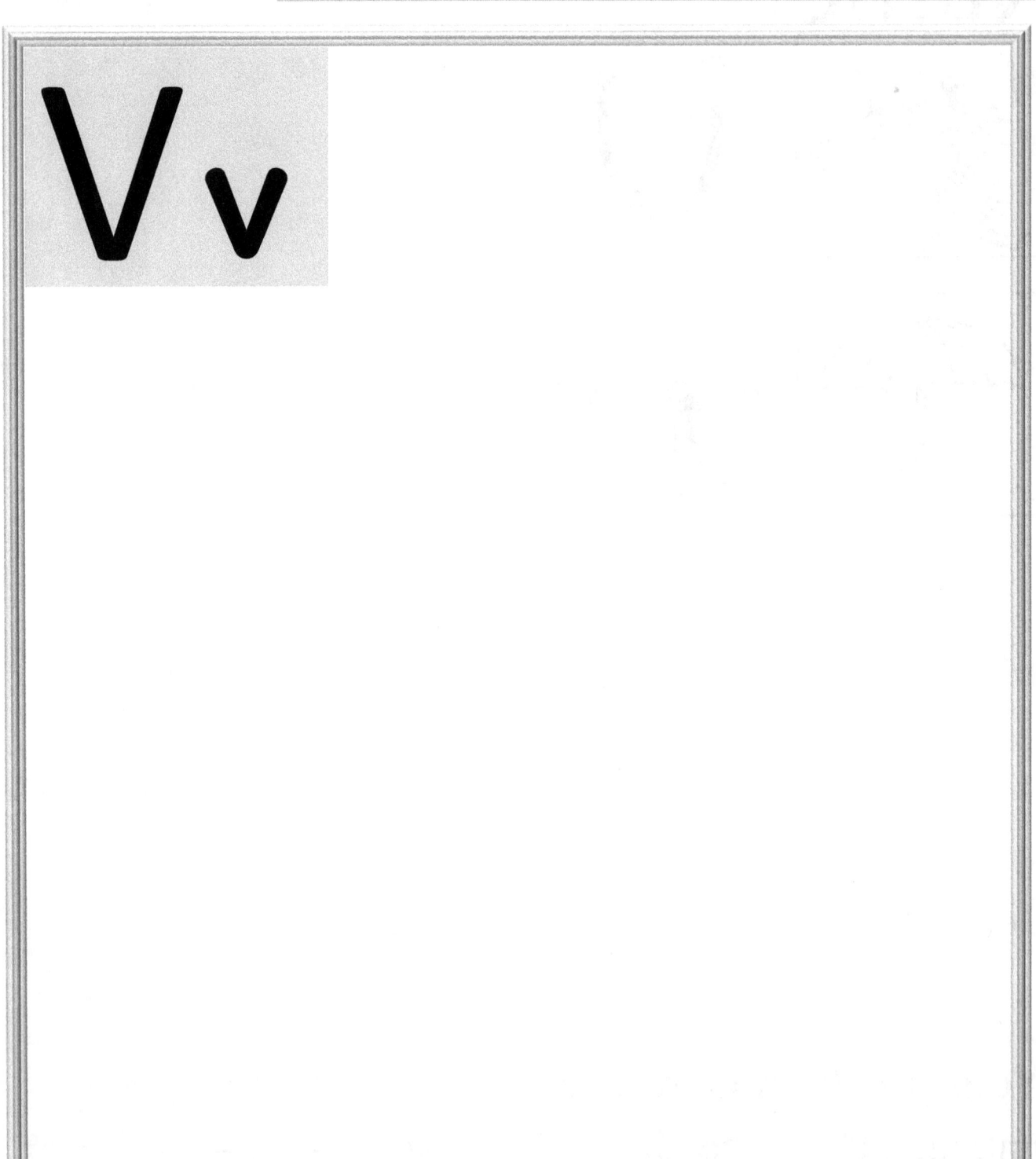

Use stick glue to glue one or more pictures of the letter and/or things that begin with the letter from packages, magazines, or online resources.

Name: _____

Color the letters. Then find the pictures at the back of the book that begin with the letter. Color the pictures and use stick glue to glue the pictures onto the squares.

A B C D E F G H I J K L M

V v

Vinny **V**ulture loves his vegetable soup very much.

N O P Q R S T U V W X Y Z

Name:

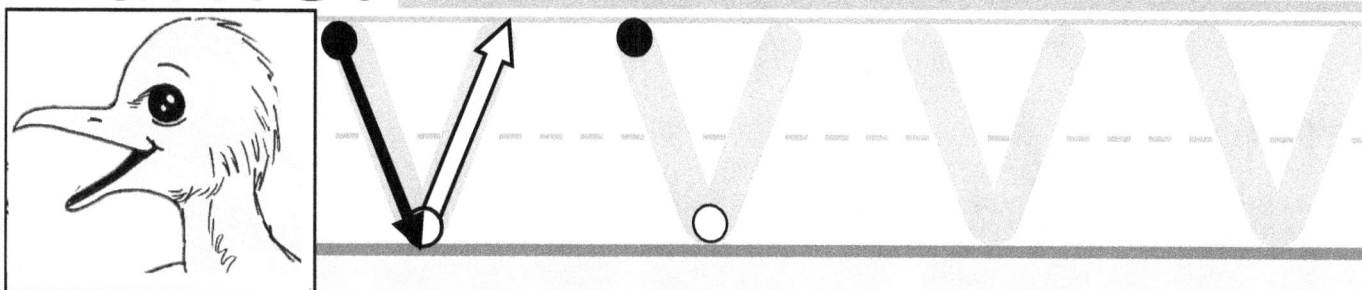

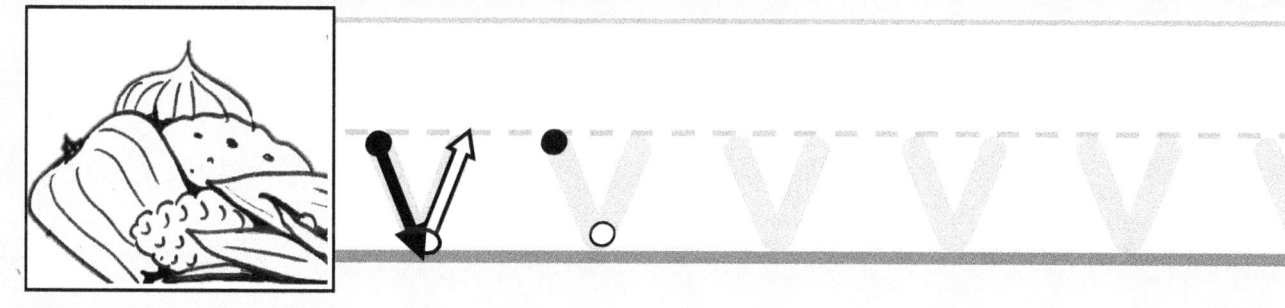

A friend gave Vinny a vase of flowers.
What would you give Vinny?
I would give Vinny _____

Complete the sentence.

Name: ⎯⎯⎯⎯⎯⎯⎯⎯⎯⎯⎯⎯⎯⎯⎯⎯⎯⎯⎯⎯⎯⎯⎯⎯⎯⎯

Use stick glue to glue one or more pictures of the letter and/or things that begin with the letter from packages, magazines, or online resources.

Name:

Ww

Color the letters. Then find the pictures at the back of the book that begin with the letter. Color the pictures and use stick glue to glue the pictures onto the squares.

A B C D E F G H I J K L M

Ww

Wendy Whale eats watermelon on the waves.

N O P Q R S T U V W X Y Z

Name: _____

 W W W W W

 w w w w w

1. **W**ho ate the fruit?

_____ ate the fruit.

2. **W**hat fruit did she eat?

She ate _____.

3. **W**here did she eat it?

She ate it on the _____.

4. **W**hen did she eat it?

She ate it in the daytime.

Name:

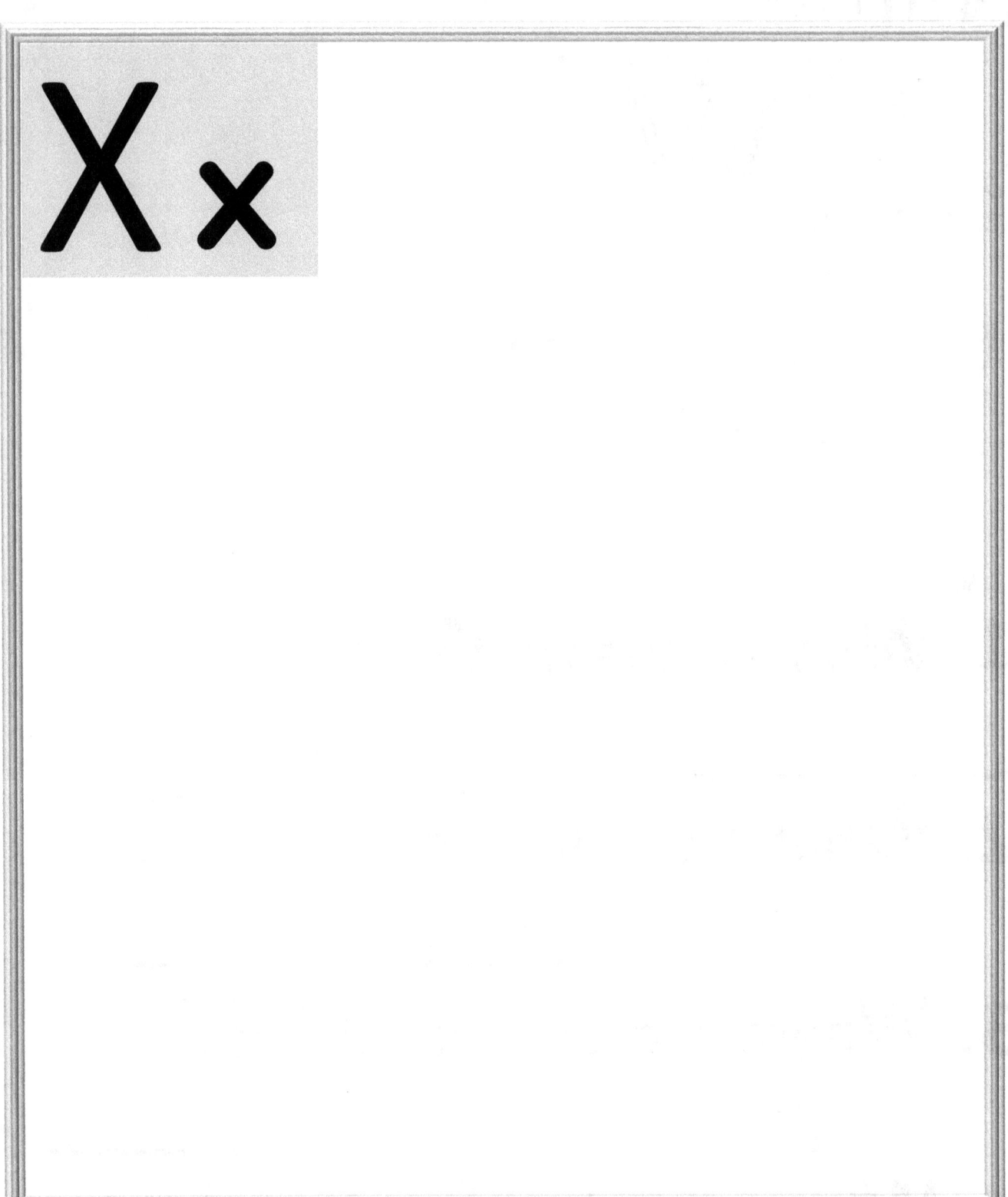

Use stick glue to glue one or more pictures of the letter and/or things that begin with the letter from packages, magazines, or online resources.

Name:

Xx

Color the letters. Then find the pictures at the back of the book that begin with the letter. Color the pictures and use stick glue to glue the pictures onto the squares.

A B C D E F G H I J K L M

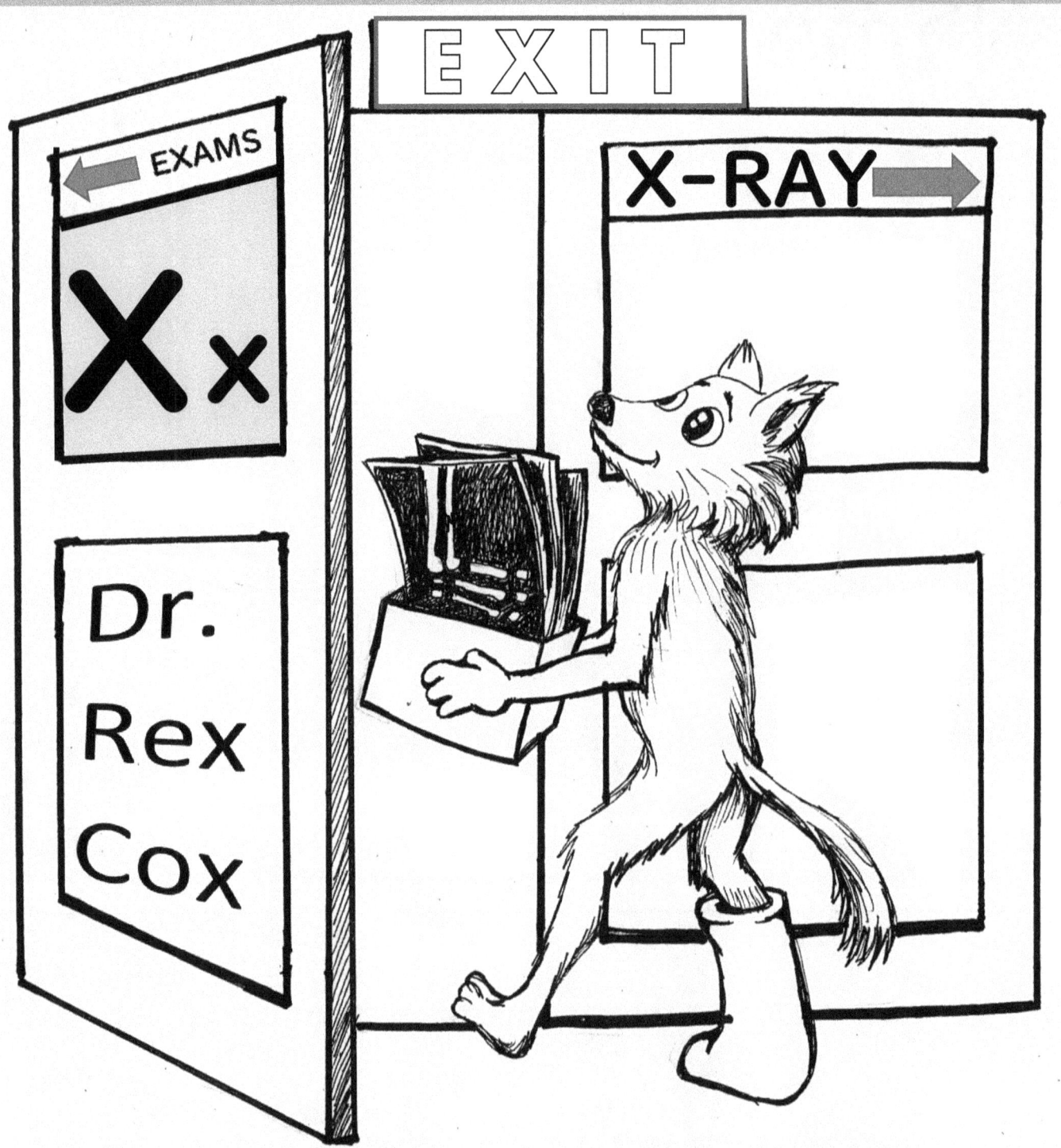

Xavier **F**ox exits with his X-rays in a box.

N O P Q R S T U V W X Y Z

Name:

X X X X X

x x x x x

X x

Xavier hurt his leg. He
went to Dr. Cox to fix his
leg. Now he feels better.

Xavier is holding his

X-ray.

Name:

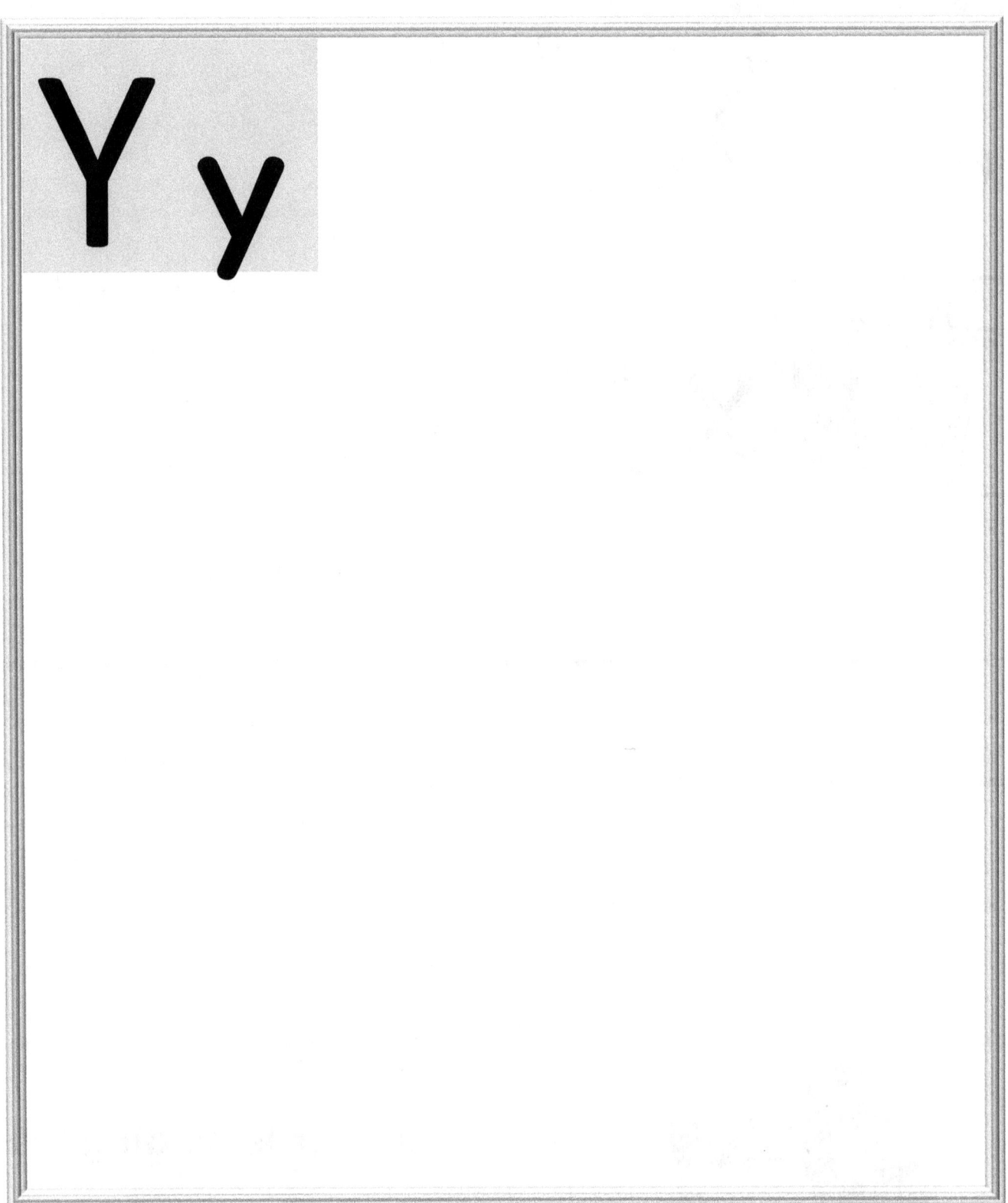

Use stick glue to glue one or more pictures of the letter and/or things that begin with the letter from packages, magazines, or online resources.

Name: _____

Color the letters. Then find the pictures at the back of the book that begin with the letter. Color the pictures and use stick glue to glue the pictures onto the squares.

ABCDEFGHIJKLM

Y y

Yanus **Y**ak is yelling too loudly in the yellow flowers!

N O P Q R S T U V W X Y Z

Name:

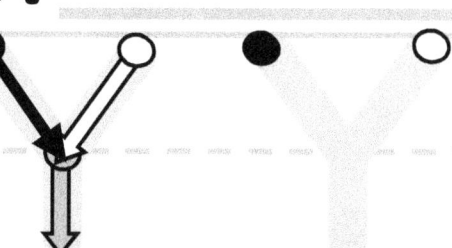

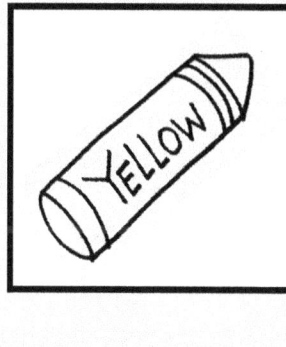

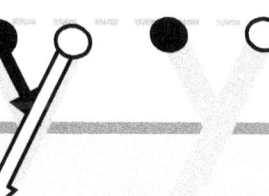

Y Y Y Y

y y y y

"I love my yellow flowers!" Yanus yelled. "Do you like my yellow flowers?" Yes or No

Name:

Z z

Use stick glue to glue one or more pictures of the letter and/or things that begin with the letter from packages, magazines, or online resources.

Name:

Color the letters. Then find the pictures at the back of the book that begin with the letter. Color the pictures and use stick glue to glue the pictures onto the squares.

A B C D E F G H I J K L M

Zz ZOO

Zig-Zag Zipper Day!

Zeze and Zack Zebra went to the zoo. They wore a lot of zig-zags and zippers!

N O P Q R S T U V W X Y Z

Name:

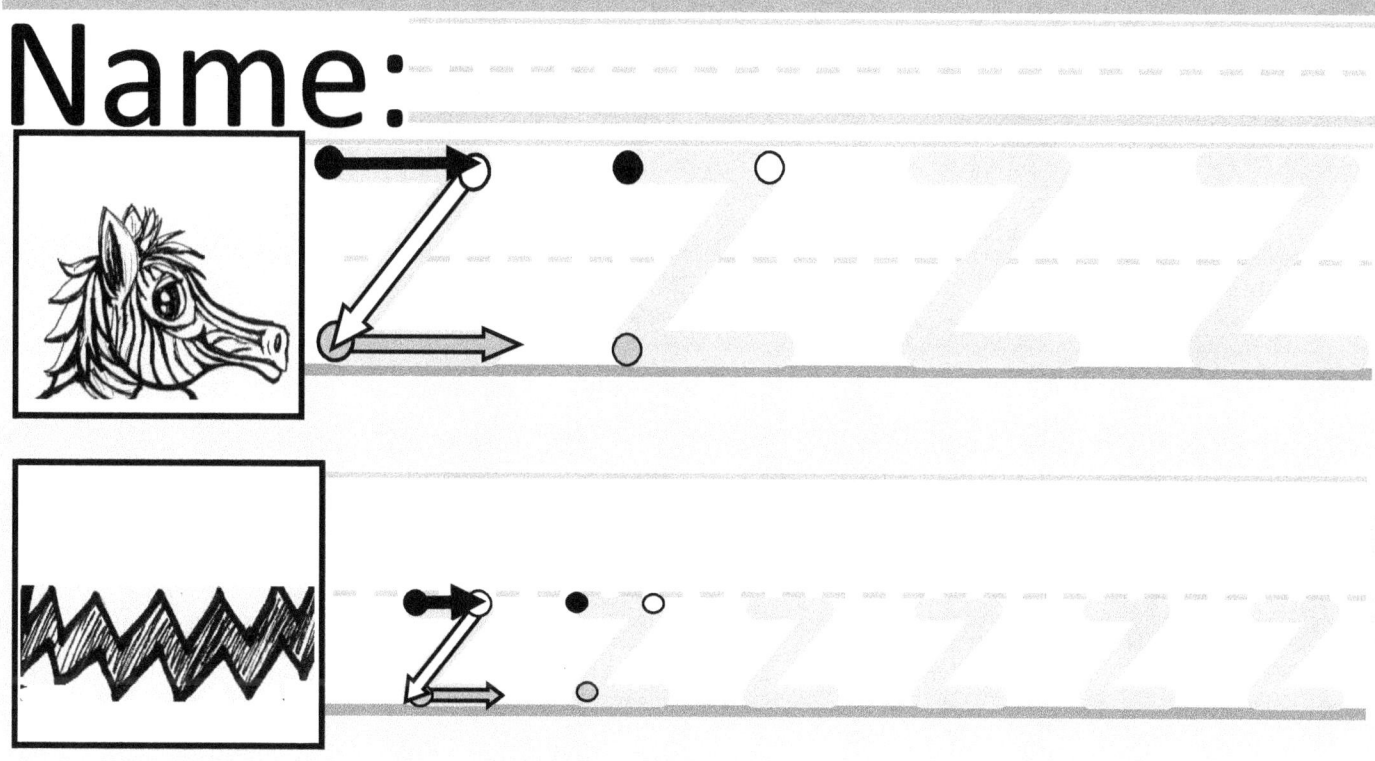

How many zippers did Zeze wear?

How many zippers did Zack wear?

Who wore more zippers?

Who wore more zig-zags?

110

name:

zero: 0 0 0

one: 1 1 1

two: 2 2 2

three: 3 3 3

four: 4 4 4

0

five: 5 5

six: 6 6

seven: 7 7

eight: 8 8

nine: 9 9

ten: 10

Name:

A B C D

E F G H

I J K L

M N O P

Q R S T

U V W X

Y Z ! ?

Name:

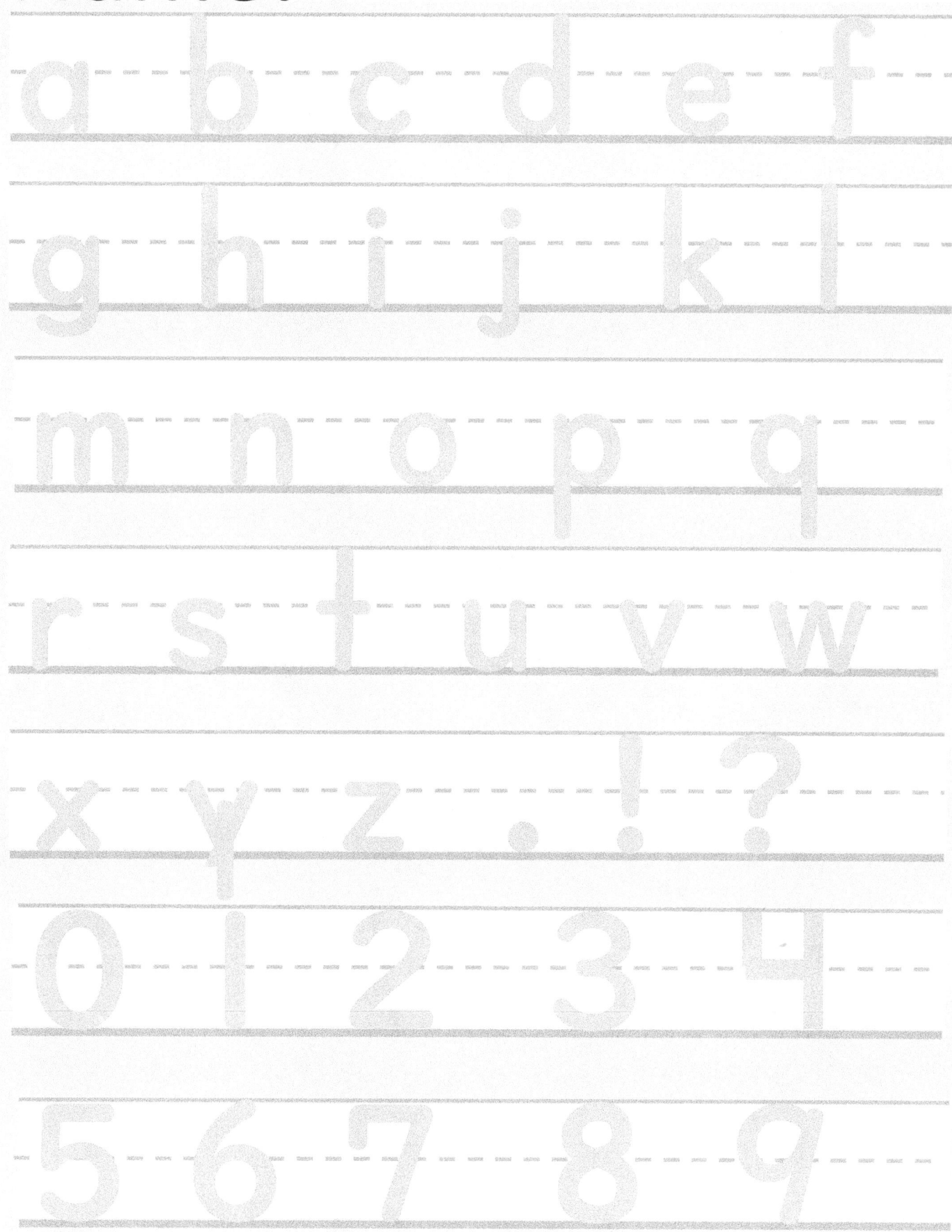

(cover)

Common Words Lists/Booklet

The Word List (p. 61-63) includes most of the words used in this book that are not included in the ABC Lists (p. 64-67). Students ages 4 and up should learn only one set at a time- at their own pace.

The numbered sets can be cut out, laminated, stapled together to form a booklet, or hole punched in the top left corner and put onto a book ring.

1
a

and

ate

all

2
be

before

best

can

3
come

did

do

does

4
for
friend
gave
get

5
give
go
got
grow

6
has
have
her
his

7
has
have
her
his

8
it
lot
love
many

9
me
my
no
not

10	**11**	**12**
of	the	which
on	to	with
or	under	yes
so	went	you

Use the following blank spaces to add any other commonly used words.

13	**14**	**15**

ABC Lists/Booklet

ABCs

_____
name

LeRoyMacPublishingHouse

(cover)

A a
alligator
ant
apple
and

B b
ball
blue
boat
brown

C c
cake
carrot
cat
cookies

D d
dog
donuts
draw
duck

E e
eat
ear
egg
elephant

F f
face
feet
fish
fun

G g
goat
grapes
grass
green

H h
happy
hat
he
horse

I i
ice
in
inch
is

J j
jam
jelly
jellyfish
juice

K k
kangaroo
keep
key
kite

L l
lemon
like
lion
lollipop

M m
make
monkey
mouse
muffins

N n
neck
necklace
nice
nose

O o
ocean
octopus
oranges
out

P p
pig
pink
popcorn
purple

Q q
quail
quiet
quilt
queen

R r
rabbit
rain
ran
red

S s
sandwich
snack
snake
sock

T t
teeth
tiger
together
turtle

U u
umbrella
under
unicorn
up

V v
vase
vegetable
very
vulture

W w
water
wave
whale
what

X x
box
exit
fox
X-ray

Y y
yak
yell
yellow
yes

Z z zig-zag zip zipper zoo	**ABC Mini Booklet** Directions for mini ABC booklet or flash cards: - Student or teacher/parent may color the pictures on each mini page. - Cut out the mini pages - Staple pages together - Students trace letters - May be laminated for wipe-off repeated use.

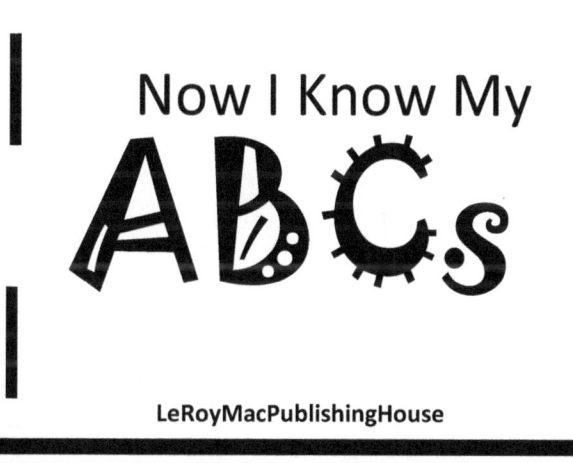

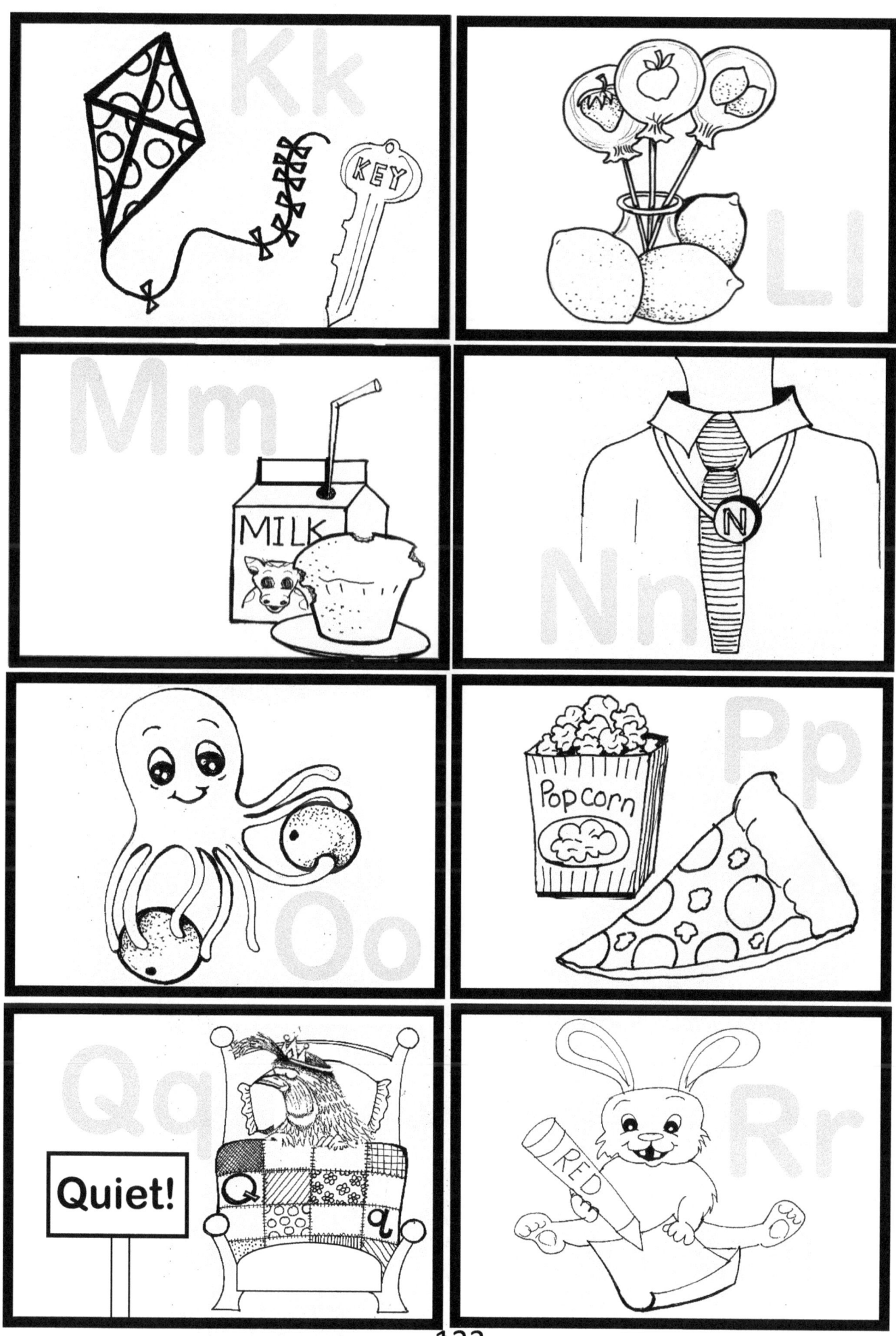

Pages 72-79 are extra pages for practicing handwriting.

- Parent/teacher may add words or letters to be traced or allow student to write words/letters/names and add their own pictures.
- Parent/teacher may ask or write a question to be answered on the page through independent writing or through tracing.
- Parent/Teacher may help the student compile a list.
- Student may draw pictures about their writing.
- Pages may be removed and laminated to use as wipe-off practice pages or in classroom/home writing centers.

Ideas for extra writing practice.

- Write words for and draw favorite foods/animals/toys.
- Animal book search. Example: Which animal in this book has a blue ball? Student may use these pages to write the answers from the book.
- Write or trace titles/words/pictures from favorite books.
- Word search. Example: Write the words from labels of favorite foods.
- Tasty Words. Write the words from lunch item packages.
- Write or copy words of a category, such as feelings or fruit.
- Write or copy outside/inside words.
- Write words or character names from a favorite movie.
- Write names, jobs, favorite items of family members or friends. (Use pictures of family/friends.)
- For centers: Place pages, crayons, and pencils on a table for small groups to copy words and draw pictures from various safe-to-handle items. Items can be theme based or random collections. Ex: cereal boxes, canned goods, candy wrappers, toy boxes, doll clothes or t-shirts with writings or slogans, cleaned drink containers, magazine cutouts, or picture books.
- Page 79 may also be used to challenge students with items to sort or find during a scavenger hunt.

a b c d e f g h i j k l m n o p q r s t u v w x y z
A B C D E F G H I J K L M N O P Q R S T U V W X Y Z

Name:

abcdefghijklmnopqrstuvwxyz
ABCDEFGHIJKLMNOPQRSTUVWXYZ

Name:

abcdefghijklmnopqrstuvwxyz
ABCDEFGHIJKLMNOPQRSTUVWXYZ

Name:

Name:

131

Teaching Suggestions:

Keep all instruction stress-free. Allow the student to make and correct mistakes while progressing at their own pace. Repeat pages when needed for sustained learning. (Laminate pages for wipe-off use or for use as a classroom center.)

If your student is...

- just learning the alphabet and how to hold a writing instrument:

- Go over no more than two letters at a time.
- Say the alphabet while pointing to each letter at the top of the pages.
- Point to the big letter on the odd-numbered page. Then find it in the line at the top of the page.
- Point to and say the names of the objects and animals drawn on the page.
- Read the sentence.
- Hold the student's hand in the correct writing position (if needed) while filling in the name section.
- Point to and say the letters on the page.
- Help the student trace the first letters on each line using the simpler handwriting guide.
- Ask the question at the bottom of the page. Help the student answer the question.
- Give the student a light-colored crayon or colored pencil to trace the letters
- Allow the student to trace and color however they chose.
- Use the same two letters at least twice. For repeated practice, use a darker crayon or pencil during the next practice time. Allow the student to "read" the sentence during the repeat practice.
- Allow student to color pictures. Keep it stress-free and the student will learn to enjoy learning!

-able to recognize most of the alphabet and properly use a writing instrument:

- Go over no more than three letters at a time.
- Have the student point to and say the letter. Then have the student find the letter in the line at the top of the page and circle it.
- Have the student say the alphabet at the top of the pages while pointing to each letter. Hold the student's hand and assist if needed.
- Have the student describe what is in the picture, then read the sentence while pointing to each word.
- Write the student's name on the correct line. Have the student trace the name.
- Have the student point to the letters under the name section while using the words "capital" or "lowercase" and the sound each time.
- Use the pictures before the letters to explain that capital letters are used to start names and sentences.
- Have the student trace the letters with a light crayon or colored pencil. Encourage them to "stay on the road" while tracing. Encourage them to stay on the white area when writing letters independently.
- Read the question with the student. Compare the punctuation at the end of sentences (period/question mark/explanation mark), or quotation marks within the sentences. Have the student trace the question and follow the directions.
- Allow the students to color the pictures.

-able to recognize the alphabet and some words, as well as write most letters:

- Go over no more than three letters at a time.
- Help the student read aloud the sentences on pages to be completed and pages already completed.
- Use any of the steps above as needed. (Always go over complete directions before giving independent work.)
- Allow the student to work independently with pencil and/or colored pencils.
- Check the student's work. Gently correct mistakes. Allow the student to correct/repeat work. Use darker colored pencils or crayons, if necessary, on repeat work. Allow the student to color the pictures.

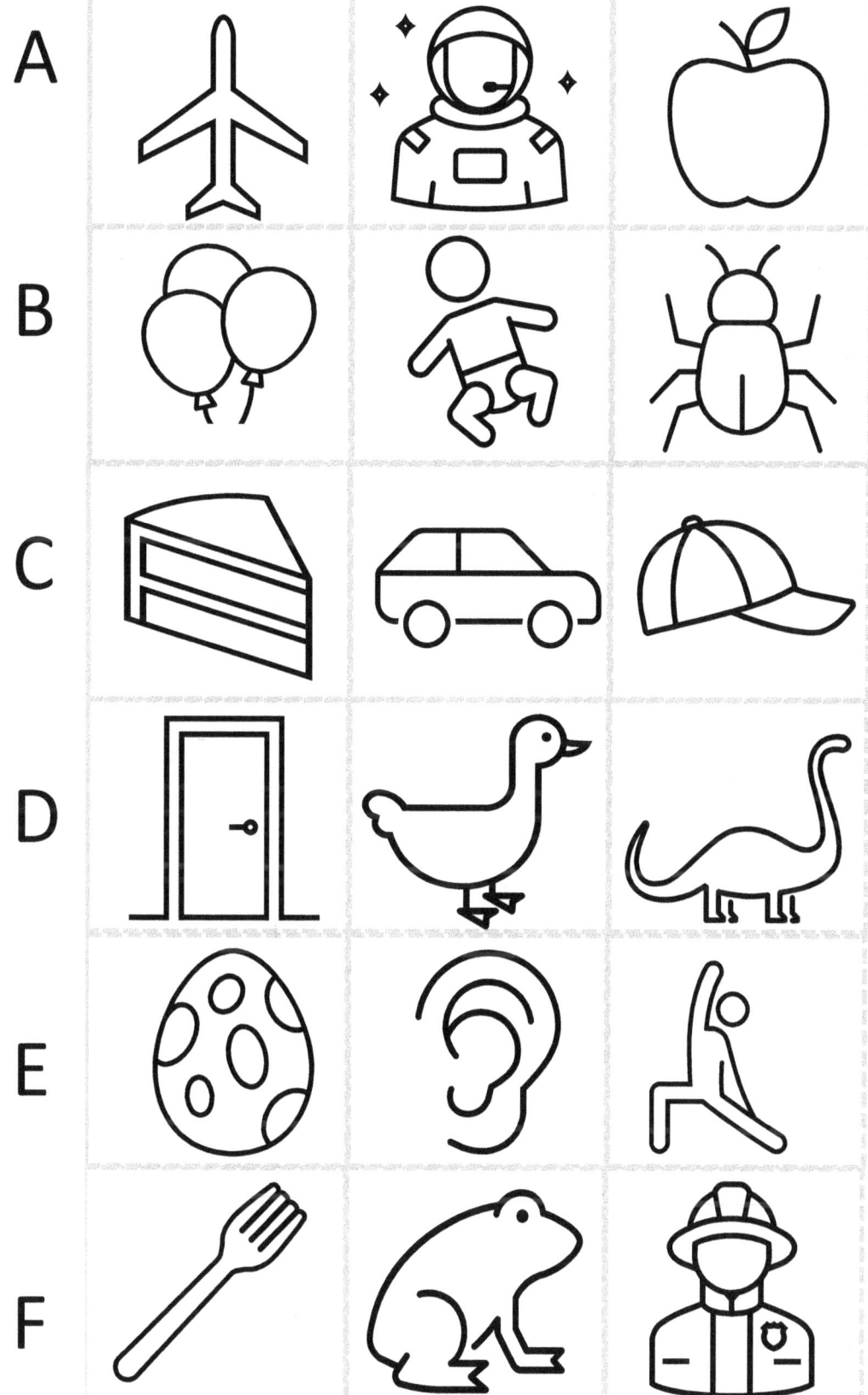

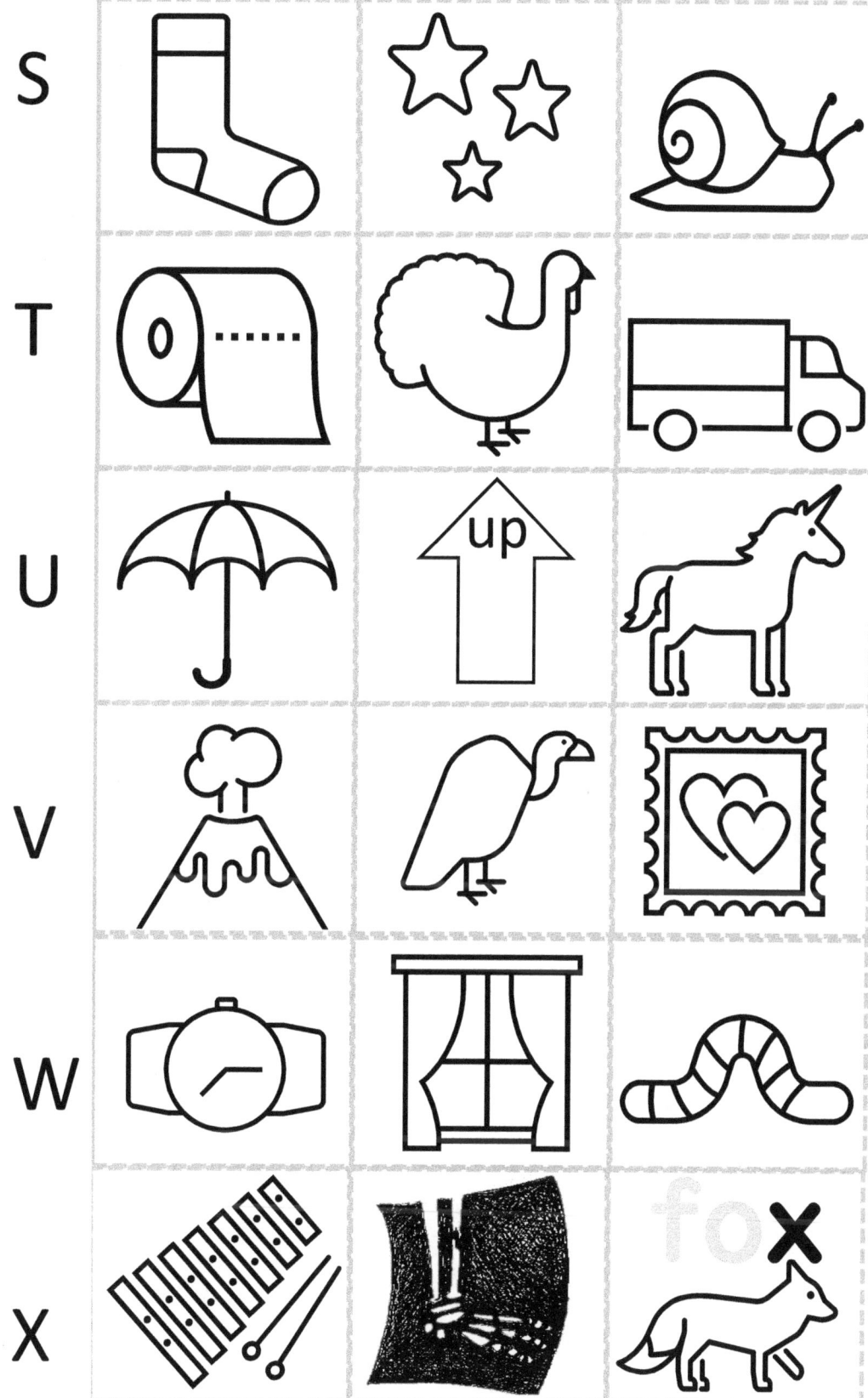

Y

Z

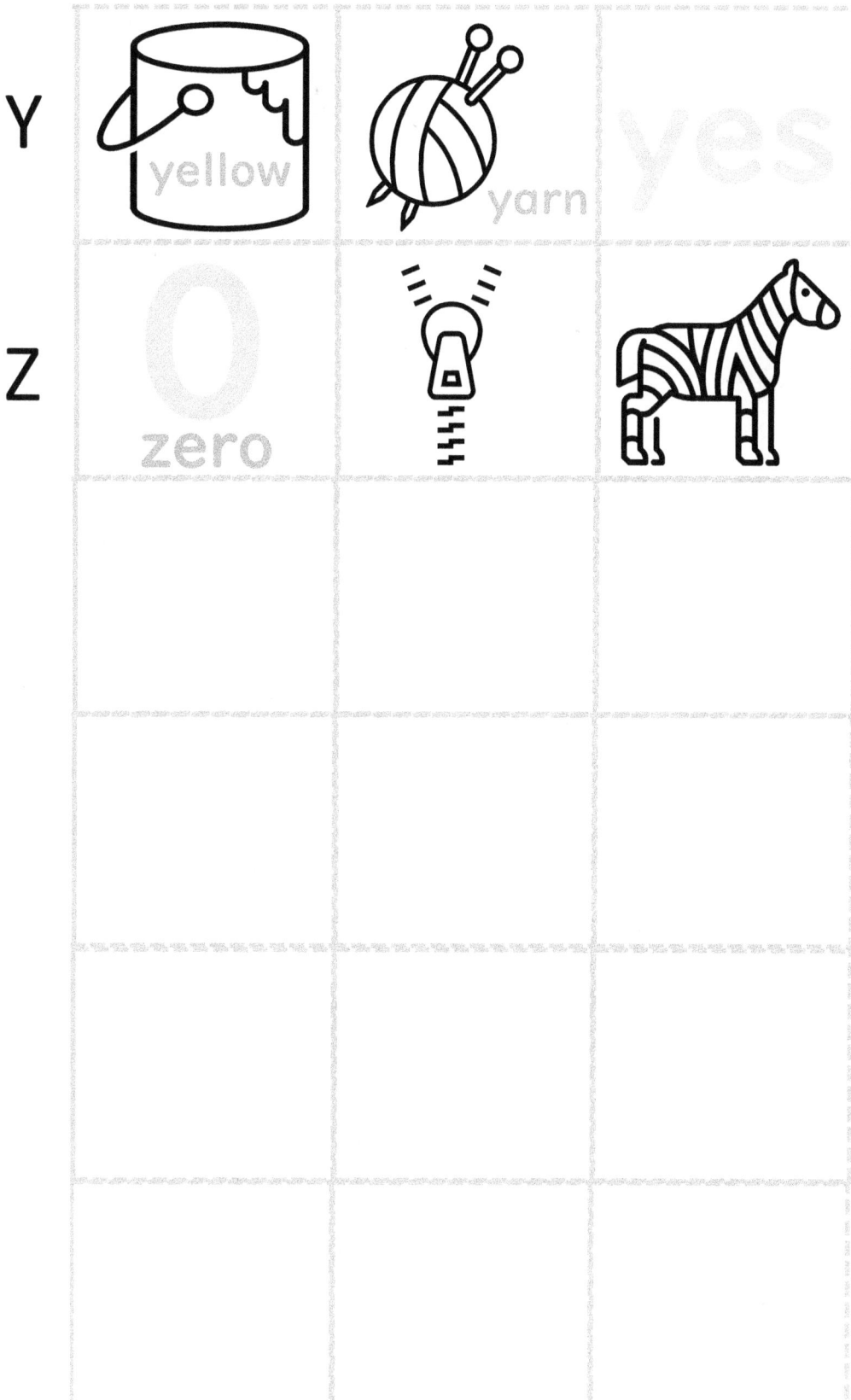

www.ingramcontent.com/pod-product-compliance
Lightning Source LLC
Chambersburg PA
CBHW081013040426
42444CB00014B/3191